LYRICS
OF MY LIFE

LYRICS OF MY LIFE

My Journey with Family, HIV, and Reality TV

BRANDEN JAMES

Published in the United States by Cleis Press, an imprint of Start Mid-night, LLC, 221 River street, 9th floor, Hoboken, NJ 07030.

Printed in the United States.
Cover design: Allyson Fields
Cover photo: Michael Dar
Text design: Frank Wiedemann

First Edition.
10 9 8 7 6 5 4 3 2 1

Trade paper ISBN: 978-1-62778-292-0
E-book ISBN: 978-1-62778-505-1

Names and identifying details have been changed throughout the book to protect personal privacy

My initial audition for *America's Got Talent* was in Chicago in 2013. I was exhausted from a recent trip home from Sydney, Australia, and I had to work that day—a matinee performance of Puccini's *La Bohème* at Lyric Opera of Chicago. I finished up around four p.m., and my jet lag was in full force. There was nowhere I wanted to be but home in my bed. But I kept hearing my partner's voice ringing over and over in my head. He'd told me on the flight home from Oz as I was fretting about whether or not to attend the audition, "If you don't audition for anything, you're never going to get anything." Obvious advice, it seems, but still I absorbed it as if it were a prophetic teaching that nobody had ever thought of before.

I arrived in a taxi at the convention center in Chicago, paid the cab, set foot on the ground, and immediately tripped and fell. Brushing off my pants, I also tried to brush off the nerves that were making me clumsy. When I arrived, the line outside wasn't too long. I only suffered anxiously for a bit in line before entering the massive convention center.

When I walked in, the sensation was all too familiar: It wasn't the first time I'd attended a cattle call for a reality television show. In my early twenties, I'd attended *American Idol* auditions at the Cow Palace in San Francisco. I repeated that experience in my late twenties at the Rose Bowl in Pasadena with my mother in tow. In my early thirties, I'd attended auditions for *The Voice* with my childhood best friend, Christina. For some unexplained reason, I was determined to get on one of those shows.

I remember having a pep talk with myself while waiting in line. I felt different this time. Perhaps it was because of the delirium and jet lag, or maybe it was my subconscious taking over. But I kept telling myself, "Be bold. Be brave." Finally, I made it into the holding room with the masses of other competitors, where the view was slightly more colorful than I anticipated. *America's Got Talent* is not just a competition for singers, but a variety show where any talent of any age and walk of life can compete against one another. There were acrobatic duos, jugglers, drag queens, contortionists, guitarists, dance troupes, and anyone else who could perform with limited equipment in tow.

"Welcome to season eight auditions," one young woman said. "Take this paperwork and a pen and find a quiet corner to fill it out."

I grabbed the paperwork and settled next to a troupe of gothic-looking performance artists who made their costumes from recycled material and performed dance pieces that were dedicated to environmental advocacy. I only know this because, as someone who has been in many auditions, I immediately sized up the competition around me.

I wrote furiously, worried that I wouldn't be seen that

day. I knew that part of the reason audiences loved reality competitions was because they grew to know and care about the contestants. But in order to win over the crowd, you had to have an interesting story. I had a story—I just wasn't sure I could tell it.

"Be bold. Be brave, Branden. You can do this." I must've said it ten times in my head and muttered it another twenty times under my breath.

"I've always been a singer," I wrote. "Singing is my identity, really. But I've obstructed my own success by getting in my own way. The truth is, I'm so full of guilt and shame that I don't think I deserve any of this. I've been HIV positive for eight years, and I've never told anyone who wasn't considered one of my closest and dearest friends."

Needless to say, this was unfamiliar territory for me. But this was part of being bold and brave. I turned in the paperwork, and approximately thirty minutes passed. As I sat there, shifting and watching the other contestants practice, my thoughts were unproductive: *How many singers have they actually heard today? I don't have a chance. What am I doing here? I should go home and be with my partner and my puppy.*

My palms became sweaty, and I noticed heat seeping out of my warm clothes. This was the typical nervous rush I have always experienced whenever I'm making myself vulnerable in front of others. For me, vulnerability could be as simple as raising my hand to ask a question in a group of strangers, or being given a stage direction in an opera rehearsal that would leave my colleagues' eyes watching to see how I moved, walked, or sang. To others, this would be a normal part of life, but to someone like me, someone without an ounce of confidence, it felt like a dissection—an invasion.

A few more minutes passed, though it seemed like an eternity. Most of the room had cleared out by this time. Finally, a man working for the show said, "Please come with me." I gathered my things: my backpack, my jacket, my phone charger, my headphones, and my dignity. I stood up and immediately felt light-headed, as if I had low blood sugar. *Chalk it up to nerves*, I thought. *Or jet lag.* My mouth was dry. I couldn't imagine having to sing anytime in the near future. I had barely gotten through *La Bohème* earlier in the day.

I peered down to the first level of the convention center, and I could see people walking toward the exit. Some were hanging their heads in disappointment, and others audibly screamed on their way out. Based on their cackles, I assumed they were teenage girls who had received good news after their auditions. The floors were a hard-tiled surface, like what you'd see in a department store, and there were large glass windows and beams everywhere, so the whole place was an echo chamber of sound. It was obvious who was given good news and who was given a disappointing "Try again next year."

I took a deep breath. I was about to share an incredibly private part of myself with a room full of perfect strangers. It was my first journey into authenticity, a giant breakthrough for me. My name is Branden James. I am an openly gay, openly HIV-positive, married Christian man. And this is my life story.

CHAPTER
ONE

I was born on June 19, 1978. An older friend of mine named Helen—an aristocratic, Oklahoma-born woman with a wicked sense of humor—recently slapped me upside my left shoulder and said, "Quit telling people your age. It is none of their damned business." I suppose there is an age stigma in showbiz. But in this world of information, it's easy to go to my Wikipedia page and find out the truth. Additionally, lying about my age just doesn't go along with my belief that it's my calling to be transparent and live a life of authenticity. My sincere apologies, Helen, but the cat is out of the bag.

I was a morning baby who came out of my mother's womb around 9:05 a.m. She says she had an immense peace about her when I was delivered. There was no pain, nor discomfort—only sheer feelings of bliss and joy. Perhaps it was because she listened to Carole King and James Taylor when she was pregnant, and I was just super chilled out. Or maybe it's because I've always had a sense of ease about me.

I was born in Tustin, California, and raised in the adjacent city of Anaheim—about two miles from Disneyland, which soon became my second home as a child, as it was for my two older brothers. My mom had a high school friend, Rick Steele, who became senior vice president at the park, and in those days she could just call Rick and he'd walk us in for free whenever we wanted. I was the type of kid who would twirl his way down Main Street, USA, singing songs from *The Sound of Music* at the top of my lungs. My parents would take us for dessert at the Carnation restaurant at the Magic Kingdom at night, and I preferred to order a salad with blue cheese dressing instead. I was always different— right from the start. I had a good childhood, from what I can remember, albeit confusing at times.

I want to remind you that these chapters are written from the perspective of a gay child, a gay teenager, and a gay forty-year-old, HIV-positive man. I find it important to add this caveat because one's identity *does* change one's perspective on life. There may be things you read in the coming chapters that seem completely out of the norm. But I hope you will try to keep an open mind and come back to this simple idea if you start to think to yourself, "Well, that would never happen to me." Growing up as a gay kid in the eighties and nineties wasn't the easiest feat.

My childhood home was a modest, three-bedroom house at the end of a residential block. My mom was a bit of a game-show maverick and won big on *Let's Make a Deal* and then later on *The Price Is Right*. Among her earnings was a baby grand piano, which my parents ended up selling to put a down payment on their first house. Little did she know that she'd have use for the piano later in life.

Our backyard was spacious and had an avocado tree on one side and a fence lined with bamboo trees on the other.

The avocado tree was a delight for us kids, as it would bear delicious, savory fruit on a yearly basis. I ate so many avocados that I grew up believing that guacamole was a food group. In Southern California, where it's perfectly normal to have Mexican food five times a week, that belief isn't completely unfounded. There was a park area that housed a gated sewage filtration system just next to us, which we called the pump house, where we would often go and explore with the neighbor kids.

I had sexual explorations from a young age, too—with both genders. As a curious kid, I had an impulse to explore *everything*. My grandparents used to get after me for smelling anything that I put in my hands. I was needlessly inquisitive and probably drove my parents crazy asking questions. I used to think I was the only child who had sexual interludes with other kids. But as I've grown older, and brave enough to ask other adults if they had similar experiences, their answers have almost always been a resounding yes.

In those tender years of five to twelve years old, I never considered it to be unnatural, although I had the innate sense to keep it under wraps from my parents. These were very innocent things: a peep show in my bedroom closet where a school girlfriend might've shown me her underwear, or a fondle with a neighbor boy at a sleepover. I've never asked my parents if they were aware of this behavior. Maybe they were, and they realized it was just part of growing up. Or maybe they were blissfully unaware. These aren't the kinds of hindsight conversations you want to have with your parents at any age.

If I wasn't playing at the adjacent park or with neighbors, you might have found me in the liquid amber tree in front of our house. Although we were in temperate Orange County, the tree changed colors, complete with piles of falling leaves in autumn, and in the spring it bore spiked balls, which we called porker balls. Those prickly little orbs stayed through the hot summers and became small weapons when I needed to defend myself against my older brothers. I was a climber and a daredevil, which was always a source of trouble for me. I never felt that I had to observe any boundaries or safety measures, which for many children are engrained. Little did I know this tendency to dive in headfirst would follow me throughout my life.

This carefree way of living led to many accidents, which I'll walk you through as quickly as possible. I was playing out in our backyard on a hot summer day, and the sprinklers were on for our amusement. We also had a yellow Slip 'n Slide set up. As a kid, I had a dangerous habit of running with my tongue out of my mouth. That day, I slipped on the wet patio and bit my tongue very badly, which led to a speech impediment. My mom cleaned up the mess and took me to the hospital to get my tongue stitched up. I pulled the stitches out at least twice before it properly healed. I can only imagine how much fun that was for my mom. We were an uninsured family.

I also ran through a sliding glass door once. My mom had just finished cleaning the house, and the door was so clean that I didn't notice that it was actually shut. More stitches, and a permanent scar on my upper lip. When I was seven years old, I had a genius idea to get in my dad's red-and-white Volkswagen van and put it in reverse on our downward-sloped driveway. I managed to back it into our neighbor's fence across the street, luckily missing the crossfire of passing traffic. Of course, my dad had to pay for damages to the fence *and* the car.

When I was twelve years old, we, as a family, attended a Christian music concert performed by Bryan Duncan and sponsored by our newfound family megachurch. It was a chilly fall night up in Ventura County. I was sitting in the bleachers watching the concert when I noticed that I had dropped my zip-up hoodie under the bleachers. In typical carefree fashion, I put my hands in my pockets and waltzed down the recreation center steps, around the corner of the bleachers, and into the dark and dirty maze underneath to find my sweatshirt. With my hands in captivity, I tripped on one of the metal foundations of the concert seating and I fell straight on my face.

With a broken nose, I screamed in agony. I ran to my parents, and we promptly left the concert with a giant bag of ice covering my face. They claim that I refused to go to the hospital, which sounds about right. So still today, if you look closely enough, you will see that I have a crooked nose. That injury made me the recipient of a colossal amount of teasing from my brothers, who aptly named me Long Nose.

At thirteen years old, I started riding my bike to and from my school in Newbury Park. It was a short commute, maybe a mile and a half. I remember riding home one beautiful afternoon without a care in the world, and I darted out in front of an old woman who was driving an ancient tank of a car. It was determined that she was speeding at thirty-five miles per hour in a twenty-five miles–per-hour zone. When she hit me, she panicked and thought I was under the car, so she threw the vehicle in reverse very quickly. It turns out I was on top of the car, so I had a second point of impact as I was rolling off the top.

I remember being in a state of shock when I realized what happened. A neighborhood lady came out of her house and rushed to see how I was. I just remember yelling out my mom's phone number and asking someone to call it. It seemed like she arrived in seconds. When we set off on the ride to Thousand Oaks hospital, my mom trailing in her car just behind, the ambulance driver craned his neck around and asked me, "Would you like to drive with the sirens on?" To which I replied, "No, I don't think so." *I refused a childhood dream to ride with sirens on in an ambulance.* I must've been in shock.

It turned out that I had broken my left ankle and femur and fractured my right ankle, elbow, and collarbone that day. I'm lucky to be alive. I wasn't wearing a helmet on that bike ride and didn't seem to learn my lesson even then, since I continued to ride helmet-free for years to come. During my recovery, I became a master at maneuvering crutches, despite all of the broken stuff. But my mastery only lasted so long. After about six weeks of recovery, I whimsically crutched my way down our steep staircase and fell, only to reinjure my leg and ankle again with fresh breaks in two places.

Then there was a traumatic fall off a cliff during my first year of college in San Francisco, complete with pins and screws in my left ankle, and more recently, a blown right eardrum from a thrill-seeking jump off a boat on Lake Las Vegas. To this day, you might find me edging on the side of a cliff in Ghost Ranch, New Mexico; Cape Town, South Africa; Diamond Head, Hawaii; or Kotor, Montenegro, in search of a perfect photo. This thrills my husband, James, the designated photographer, who has a wicked fear of heights.

———————

My parents were married fresh out of high school at nineteen years old: they were just kids. I can recall stories of how my mom's older brothers were counting the months between their marriage and their first child—my older brother Jason was born only twelve months after their wedding. It was not a shotgun wedding, as they used to say—they were just eager to have children. Things were different in the early seventies. There was still a great societal pressure for women to be the matriarch. It wasn't terribly common for women to work, and young parenthood was still a definite trend. Today, you'd be hard-pressed to find someone who didn't think it was crazy to consider bringing up a child as a teenager. But my parents were thrilled.

My father was a typical sports jock who'd come from a very atypical family. His father was a country singer who toured with Johnny Cash and played on radio shows with Elvis Presley. His family migrated to California from Iowa with my grandfather's band, Jimmy James and the Golden Rhythm Boys, while they were moving up in the music world. At some point, the band of good ol' boys got homesick, broke up, and moved back to Iowa. But my grandfather and his family stayed in California and released a few more singles. He eventually took his music earnings and bought two Mobil gas and automotive service stations and operated them until he retired.

My grandfather was a bit of a wild man in his younger

years: living a hard and fast life in the same way that Johnny Cash did. One of the biggest reasons he left music was because he didn't want to get caught up in *all of that*. It's my assumption, based on pieces of family stories I've put together, that he never used hard drugs, but he had a rather hefty drinking problem. There was never any order in my dad's family home. His mom was married to a controlling man who expected her to sit at home and wait on his every need. For a long period, she had to ask permission to leave the house and, often, my grandfather refused to let her go. She was not a skilled cook, either, which left her open to much scrutiny from her husband and three children. My dad once described one of his least favorite dinners that his mother served: tacos. These weren't tacos as we know them today. They consisted of ground beef, kidney beans, lettuce, tomato, and a delectable mixture of ketchup and mayonnaise, which his mom called salsa.

My dad's interest in music was spawned from his father's passion, although he didn't have the same dedication or flair for it. Still, he had a Gibson guitar with ivory etchings, and he used to sit us kids around the fireplace and play and sing the songs of his heroes, Elvis Presley and Johnny Cash. I knew all the words to "Johnny B. Goode" before I knew how to form a proper sentence.

My father has always been a kind and fair man with a smile on his face. He is known as a stubborn jokester who at times doesn't take life very seriously. He spent the better part of his career as a truck driver. For ten years, however, he owned his own successful business. His whole life changed when he was just forty years old—my age now. He had an aneurysm at the stem of the brain, which ruptured as a result of a congenital condition called AVM, or arteriovenous malformation.

He spent a couple of weeks in a dark room in the ICU, since he was very sensitive to light. When the time came, he was transferred to USC Medical Center and was eventually operated on. As this happened, his successful business distributorship was stripped from him by the corporate leaders of his company. Their claim was that he was expanding too quickly, with more than five hundred accounts in the greater LA basin.

After my dad's multimonth-long recovery, he went back to what he knew best: the trucking industry. Because he was unfit to drive, he tried his hand at dispatching instead, organizing the execution of deliveries for fellow truckers across the US. One of the side effects of his brain surgery was his susceptibility to seizures. Forgetful in nature as he was, he wasn't always consistent about taking his medications. He skipped a couple of doses by accident, had a seizure, fell down two flights of stairs, and emerged with bulging discs in his spine and chronic pain in his back and neck. He would later undergo shoulder and hand surgery as a result of the accident.

My dad was just my age when his wife had to become the breadwinner, when he could no longer work, exercise, or provide financially for his family. My mom was taken by surprise when she had to reenter the workforce on a full-time basis. She had no formal education, only a few classes at community college under her belt and some part-time aerobics instruction experience. Within a span of months, she added full-time caregiver, nurse, and sole income provider to her family résumé.

To say she was overwhelmed is an understatement. I was with her on several occasions when it all caught up to her. We'd just left the hospital where we were visiting my dad in order to run some typical errands: car wash, gas, and grocery shopping. My mom and I decided to get some of our favorite ice cream from Thrifty's. We left the drugstore with cones in hand, got back in the car, and headed out of the parking lot toward our house. About to make a right turn onto the main road, my mom took a quick lick of her ice cream cone before making the turn. A very impatient lady in the car behind us blared on her horn in relentless fashion for a good thirty seconds. My mom was so overwhelmed by this lady's rude behavior that she put the van in park, got out of the car, and threw the ice cream cone at her car before scampering back to the van.

The ice cream stuck to the lady's windshield and dripped down her window. The lady got out of the car and returned the favor: she scraped the cone off her windshield, waddled herself to the front of our van, and threw the cone at our windshield. My mom waited for the lady to get out of the way, put the car in gear, and burned rubber out of the parking lot. She eventually pulled over on the side of the road and started to sob hysterically while the groceries melted in the back seat.

Although these memories of my parents' hardships remain vivid in my mind, I wasn't traumatized by them, per se—I was rather occupied with my own confusion. It was my younger sister, Ashley, who was probably the most affected, having mistaken the absence of her parents as abandonment from the tender age of eight. I'm so proud of how far she's come despite her struggles: she now has a master's degree in applied behavior analysis, and she mentors individuals diagnosed with autism spectrum disorder. My middle brother, Shane, was also caught in the crossfire, suffering from teenage behavioral issues without a parent to properly guide him through the formative latter years of high school. Some of these things I believe we are predisposed to, and our parents cannot do anything about them, no matter how hard they may try.

My mom grew up in a Latin Catholic family in Los Angeles, one of six children who survived from her mother's ten pregnancies. Her father, my Grandpa De la Rosa, as we called him, was a kind and caring man who cherished his ever-expanding family. He was also a machismo ex-navy man whose mother and father were from Spain and Mexico originally. His values were controversial, to say the least. He drank and smoked heavily and was most certainly considered an alcoholic as a young father. He drove his children to excel in sports, education, and business, and he ruled my grandmother Dorothy with an iron fist.

I have striking memories of spending weekends at their house, where he would order her around as if she were some sort of indentured servant. At mealtimes he would say, "More beans, Dorothy." (Refried beans, or frijoles, were staples for breakfast, lunch, and dinner.) "More steak, Dorothy. More water, Dorothy. Dorothy, get the door. Get the phone. Goddamn it, Dorothy, what are you doing?" I had no doubt what my grandmother's name was. He reminded us ad nauseum by nagging at her.

I loved my grandfather with all of my heart, and my grandparents loved each other with great faith and conviction. It's simply that the time period they lived in was different. My grandparents were there for us kids at times my parents could not be. They provided Christmas presents for all of us in lean years when my parents couldn't afford to. During the period that my dad became debilitated, my grandparents came to stay with us kids while my parents were occupied at USC Medical Center. They helped us financially through those dark years and even provided some parenting.

My mom has played a huge role in my life and will continue to. In my early days as a toddler, I remember going with her to her aerobics classes where she was an instructor. My great-aunt Cybil was the childcare instructor at the club, and if I wasn't spending time with her in the nursery, I was in the back of my mom's class watching her teach and listening to the records of Michael Jackson, Lionel Richie, Madonna, and the soundtrack from *The Wiz*. When I was six years old, my parents bought me a yellow Fisher-Price record player. I would lock myself in my room and listen to the vinyl soundtracks of *Dumbo*, *The Fox and the Hound*, *Lady and the Tramp*, and *101 Dalmatians*. I was as obsessed with the music of Disney movies as I was with Disneyland itself. It was during this time of my life when I developed an ear and a love for music—especially pop music.

In those early days, it felt like my mom and I were best friends. My father was often traveling, sometimes five days at a time. My brothers were at school, and my sister wasn't yet but a glint in my parents' eyes. I was hooked on my mom. We'd go shopping together and run family errands. She still kept me in check, but in fun ways. I remember saying shortly after we'd eaten a big meal, "Mom. I'm hungry," to which she would reply, "I'm Lynda, it's nice to meet you."

With that said, I was always thrilled when my dad walked through the door. He had it easy in some ways: he was gone a fair amount, so he'd always be in the limelight when he was at home. I'd run to the door and yell, "Daddy!" and he'd pick me up and give me a big hug and a kiss on the lips. He was such an affectionate man with all of us.

We are blessed to come from a lineage of great genes, and all six of us James family members know that in some capacity. There's no shortage of good looks at our De la Rosa family get-togethers. My uncles, aunts, and cousins have always been striking to look at. For my siblings and I, we didn't exactly have to seek out people who were attracted to us—they came flocking to us. When you're good-looking, whether it be in your developing years or as a late-blossoming silver fox or ageless cougar, people treat you differently.

For as long as I've been aware of attraction, I've been on the receiving end of this, seen differently by classmates, relatives, family, friends, colleagues, teachers, and professors. In order to make up for my lack of self-esteem, I thrived on the idea that everyone thought I was handsome. To this day, I still check myself out in the mirror with a sort of narcissistic admiration. It's a hard habit to break when I've been doing it my whole life. Mind you, I did have an awkward teenage phase from about fourteen to sixteen, when I was anything but attractive. Carrying over the blond banged hair of my childhood, I had a full set of braces on my teeth, and my head was too big for my scrawny body. I had no idea how to dress myself, and my geeky interests in cooking, language, film, and music were rare for someone my age.

Of course, there were other attributes the James kids had

to offer other than our inherited good looks. Aside from excelling in sports, Jason was extremely intelligent and well spoken. As the oldest sibling, he had a sense of duty to look after the rest of us. I remember him being a warm and caring brother. Shane was a beautiful soul with a big heart but always had a frail emotional resilience that sometimes got him into trouble.

My baby sister was last in the birth order. Her name is Ashley. She arrived on this planet the morning of January 19, 1985, just hours before my great-grandfather Patrick O'Connell died and a week after my great-aunt Mildred passed away. Ashley was released from the hospital with a high risk of SIDS, so when she first came home, she had a monitor on her that would beep every time she rolled over. I remember hearing Mom's bloodcurdling scream when she received a phone call about her favorite aunt Mildred's passing, just a week after she'd given birth. I can only imagine my mom enduring that sort of emotional stress, coupled with common postnatal depression and a husband back on the road.

But my sister, without ever trying, provided calm and comfort for everyone in our family. She was the baby girl my mom had prayed for after bearing three boys, and she lit up the room with her smile and fiery personality everywhere she set foot. She had arbitrary cravings for Popsicles and lipstick, which she referred to in her toddler jabber as "possilo" and "lutut." We often found her in my mom's room having raided her makeup bag, with a half-eaten tube of pink lipstick, which had also been smeared onto her face. If you're going to eat lipstick, I guess you may as well use it to paint your face as well.

She was the princess we'd all been waiting for. Ashley and I shared a room in the front of our house, and my mom bought my sister and me matching Cabbage Patch dolls. Mine was a boy named Fritz Patrick; Ashley had a girl doll named Hannah Joy. Our love for Cabbage Patch Kids was just one of the many things we had in common. Despite the disagreements my siblings and I have had over the years, there is always love when they're around.

My sister was my savior in many ways. We took baths together and laughed and cuddled and cried together. We dressed up her Barbie dolls and braided the tails of the horses in her My Little Pony collection. Ashley was an extension of me. She was my true friend and ally, and I longed for her to be everywhere I was. I wonder if my older brothers played with girl dolls or dressed up in their best friends' dresses. I doubt it. I would love to know what my mom thought of it. Maybe she didn't think anything of it.

Jesus was like the seventh member of our family. My dad famously tells the story that my mom wouldn't marry him unless he became a Christian. She was saved on the beach in Corona del Mar, California. It was a huge point of contention among her family—she was a seventeen-year-old convert from Catholicism to evangelical Christianity. I can't blame her for making a change; it was a much more uplifting and social way to go to church, and the music was more accessible. Giving your life to God and accepting Jesus Christ as your personal lord and savior can be supremely liberating. According to the doctrine of this style of Christianity, you are free from sin and have been forgiven eternally and granted a pass into heaven, essentially.

We went to church every Sunday. We were creationists

who faithfully believed man was born out of the rib of Adam and the forbidden fruit of Eve. My parents sacrificed everything they had to keep paying our private school tuition at a Lutheran elementary school. Looking back, I'm not sure how they did it, to be honest. I remember there were many nights when dinner was Kraft macaroni and cheese and applesauce: an economical meal and a kid's delight.

Us boys all played soccer and baseball. I never excelled in these sports, so there was a period when my parents enrolled me in gymnastics, which was more my style. Still, when it came time for competition, I would sit in my parents' van and cry, refusing to go in and battle with the other gymnasts. My older brothers went on to play football. I quit a week after hell week: the two-week period in which you have the most grueling training you could imagine. My siblings, especially my sister, were the sports stars in the family. I found the whole thing to be laborious, and I never understood why people cared so much about this style of competition.

I'd always prefer to go to the school gym and play on the damaged piano that was hiding in the back corner rather than play sports in the schoolyard. I knew I was different as a kid. But I didn't put the pieces together until I was about thirteen years old.

As puberty took hold, I had a particularly arousing dream about my classmate Dan, who was my desk mate in my global science class. When I woke up from that dream, I felt guilty for having those strange, homosexual thoughts. I knew it was sinful, but as much as I felt culpable, I also felt safe. It was as if, for the first time, I'd discovered a piece of my true identity. As for Dan, the classmate, he had no idea, nor did he share my feelings. He was a dude in every sense of the word; in fact, I didn't find him attractive when I step back and think about it. Dreams transport us to the subconscious, and what we dream about isn't necessarily what we hold as truth in our conscious lives.

Eventually, the draw to my classmate waned, and my attention moved on to other boys at school. My attraction to other boys started occupying most of my thoughts. I was easily infatuated with good-looking fellas at school and found them charming and enticing in a way I'd never experienced with a girl. I couldn't wait for certain classes, where I could interact with particular boys, and I purposely formed friendships with some of the guys I had crushes on.

It was at thirteen when I was fully aware of my sexuality. And at that point, I set about hiding everything emotional and physical, for fear it was transparent. I think my choice to hide my sexuality was instinctual. I'd been on the playground at school long enough to hear words like *faggot* and *fairy* tossed around. Both girls and boys would say things like, "Ew. That's so gay." Or, "Don't do that, you look like a girl." I remember a day when I was in the seventh grade, and there was meant to be a heat wave the next day. To prepare for the hot weather, I chose a pair of multicolored, striped short shorts with a Velcro crotch to wear to school. My mom and I had some words that morning when I got ready. She insisted that I change into a different pair of shorts. I insisted on wearing them to school, and because I was just one of four kids she had to shuffle off to class, I won the battle.

Sure enough, within minutes of my first-period computer class, my friend Andrew Chan started singing that

stupid song—"She wears short shorts." Some other classmates chimed in and laughed along, until they were eventually hushed by our computer lab instructor. I reached in
my backpack and pulled out my oversize, black-and-yellow
hoodie and put it on. It covered just enough of my legs to
make the shorts disappear. I'm not sure what was worse,
because after the transformation, it appeared as if I wasn't
wearing anything at all from the waist down. First period
moved into second, and I was sweating underneath that
hoodie, all the while enduring shots like, "Hey, Branden!
Did you leave your pants at home?"

"Nice legs," said one kid, whistling and cackling. "Why
are you dressed like a girl?"

I spent that day in the library and got lost in a book to
take my mind off the ridicule. It would have taken a lot to
get me into the library during a lunch break in those days.
I loved the outdoors, and I wasn't much of a reader. Still,
the book was the perfect companion and a disguise to my
loneliness.

I did have one secret weapon as a kid, and that came
in the form of intelligence. I won the school spelling bee
in both seventh and eighth grades, and it forced many of
my classmates to respect me a little more. At the end of
the day, I didn't have to do *too* much hiding to blend in,
compared to some LGBTQ kids. I never had a particularly
effeminate way about me. I had a relatively deep speaking
voice and carried myself with a passable amount of traditional masculinity. My clothes were naturally oversize,
because I would inherit them from my brother. I always
pitied the kids who stood out. Unlike them, I could often
dissolve into the crowd like a chameleon when I needed to.

Thanks to my older brothers, I could pull out sports lingo when it was required and jump in on a basketball game if necessary. But I never enjoyed it. I think what made me seem different was my sensitivity. Aside from being soft-spoken, I was always attuned to the bullied kid or the special needs student. I was a sucker for the lost puppy and the down-and-out homeless person on the street. Most thirteen-year-old boys would blaze past those details like a Tasmanian devil.

At this age, I felt like I didn't belong anywhere—and belonging is something we all need as human beings. This feeling of being ostracized by my classmates led to severe childhood depression, which in turn perpetuated more lies and embellishments. I often turned to eating as a way to mask this depression. Most people would not believe, seeing me now, that I was ever an overeater, but from the age of thirteen until about twenty-three, I definitely experienced some sort of eating disorder coupled with body dysmorphia. I'll admit that I still have body shame issues. I doubt they will ever go away.

As a kid, when I sat on a chair in shorts, or on a toilet seat, my legs would fan out, and I would convince myself that I was chubby. Truth was that I had muscular legs from having been a soccer player and a gymnast, but through my clouded filter, I was fat. My eating habits were out of control. Instead of having one ice cream bar, I would eat six. And then guilt would overcome me and I would force myself to throw up. That would normally be followed by an intense run or a long bike ride, because I didn't want to get fat. This was part of a vicious cycle that would start up whenever I was in a state of depression. The cycle would consist of lying, bingeing and purging, and doing something forbidden, such as smoking a cigarette. Rinse and repeat. I don't think my parents ever noticed my heavy heart. There was too much going on in their lives, and I was a virtuoso when it came to camouflaging anything that could possibly expose the *real* me. That depression has never left—it has only worsened. I've just learned how to manage it with medication and by making healthier emotional choices.

Where *did* I belong? I wasn't sure. I couldn't tell my brothers about my sexuality. It wasn't safe to talk about it with my friends. I was ashamed, of course. In high school youth group, I was taught about what the church considered right and wrong. I remember receiving a large, fold-over pamphlet that looked like a driving map. The pamphlet talked about the other major religions and how they compared to nondenominational Christianity. Every other religion listed—Hinduism, Mormonism, Catholicism, Buddhism, Seventh-day Adventists, Christian Science—were all wrong, according to this piece of literature.

I used to listen to my dad and brothers wax poetic about the plight of the homosexual and what might happen in the afterlife to someone like me. They believed that I'd be sent to hell. I was taught that Jesus Christ was a perfect human being, and I was assured that I was eternally forgiven after I accepted Christ into my heart. But I didn't understand how I could then be sentenced to hell for something I didn't have any control of. The Jesus I came to know and understand would never punish me for being myself, would he?

CHAPTER

TWO

I t's a wild, out-of-body experience having to be guarded
from such a young age—constantly watching yourself for
any sign that might give you away or make you a target.
Think about this fact: there are only twenty-six countries in
the world where gay marriage is legal. In the 195 countries
on Earth, seventy-two of them still hold homosexuality as
illegal.[1] In some of those, death is the punishment for committing homosexual acts. And of course, in America, gay
marriage only became legal nationwide in 2015. Convicted
murderers serving out their jail sentences were allowed to
marry, as were rapists and master thieves. What message was
I to take from this growing up, except that my sexuality was
somehow a worse crime?

Can you imagine being a person who can't be themselves without fear of prison time, or who is unable to
marry the person they love? Still, to this day, I have to be

---

1 Duncan, Pamela. "Gay Relationships Are Still Criminalised in 72 Countries, Report Finds." The Guardian. July 27, 2017. Accessed May 28, 2019.
https://www.theguardian.com/world/2017/jul/27/gay-relationships-still-
criminalised-countries-report.

guarded around every new person I come across. I travel to many foreign countries for a living, and I cannot be openly gay or affectionate with my husband on those travels. I sweat bullets when we go through security in places like Papua New Guinea or the UAE, worried that they may search my bags and ask about the small pharmacy I carry on me. HIV-positive people are technically banned from entering many of the places I travel.

People ask me all the time after my shows, "Are you married? Do you have a girlfriend? Is it hard to be away from your wife?"

For a long time, I would play along with their questions and respond with things like, "It's hard. I definitely miss her, but we make it work." After a while, it became taxing to lie about myself just to spare the discomfort of an audience member. As an alternative, I've experimented in telling the truth. Many times, that hasn't gone over well. My husband, James, and I have been shunned by formerly adoring audience members who were inquisitive about our personal lives after our show. They ask twenty questions, we tell them the truth, and as soon as they hear it, they walk off and won't acknowledge us anymore.

These days, I no longer consider that a problem I am meant to take on. If we offend people simply because we're different, that's on them—not us.

But I didn't always have the benefit of that perspective. I was forced to mature early, simply because I wasn't comfortable talking about girls, and I certainly wasn't secure enough to speak openly about my preference for the same sex. My parents taught me to be true to my word, to obey *and fear* God, and to live my life with integrity, but I found myself in situations where I was constantly lying. When you have no choice but to protect yourself by lying and making questionable modifications, it shrouds you with dishonor, guilt, and shame. That describes the bulk of my formative years.

I spent so much time secluded, just trying to figure everything out in secret. When I was truly alone and safe from scrutiny, I would often act out and do something forbidden. It was an emotional outlet for me, an escape. I would lie about stupid things and exaggerate details. I would tell tales about my imagined heroism or stories about celebrity sightings. I would stretch the truth about the family vacations we went on, the money our family had, the places I'd traveled. This is a habit I carried well into my thirties. It wasn't until my husband, James, pointed it out to me one day that I finally stopped. He said, "You know, Branden, you don't have to bend the truth to impress me. I love you just as you are." If only I'd had someone like James in my life back then.

When I was alone, I tried to express myself in small bursts. I shaved the hair off my arms and legs several times and painted my nails but then removed the polish immediately for fear of getting caught. I even shaved half of my right eyebrow off one night in the bathtub. It still hasn't fully grown back, and for the longest time I was shading it in with an eyeliner pencil that I'd stolen from my mom's makeup case. I was basically screaming to the world that I was gay!

I was into taking baths and making secret use of my mom's electric body massager at the time. Once, when my parents were out of town, I took a pack of cigarettes into the bathroom, had my way with the little toy, ran a bath, and smoked the cigarettes until I was sick. Smoking was such a turn-on for me—I would get aroused when I put a cigarette in my mouth because it was so forbidden. That weekend after my smoking binge, I spent the next two days scrubbing the walls with a soft cloth and soap and water to get rid of the smell that had etched itself into the bathroom walls. I never considered the impact smoking indoors might leave on the walls; I was mostly just concerned about hiding it from my brothers.

Meanwhile, I was also hiding my true identity at school. I had two polar-opposite primary school experiences. The first was a private school, where my teachers were nurturing and the students were polite. My Lutheran school was quite a shielded environment. My older brothers attended the same school and always had my back—I felt safe there knowing what to expect and how to navigate my environment. In a faith-based school, my idiosyncrasies were less apparent. Swearing was forbidden—we were taught to uplift one another, and there was a much greater sense of community. Additionally, the Lutherans were laid-back and less guilt driven than my evangelical family church. Our required Wednesday attendance at chapel was more ceremonial than it was spiritually invasive, and our curriculum was almost entirely secular.

My third-grade teacher, Mr. Mastriano, was my first mentor and a personal friend of our family. He incorporated music in our class, piano in particular, and urged us to discover our creative selves. He was a slight man with dark curly hair who loved his students dearly. My parents were in a bind one weekend, with an unexpected out-of-town trip on the horizon, and Mr. Mastriano offered to watch us boys for the weekend. He took all three of us in and splurged on dinners and a visit to the zoo.

But when I was moved into public school at the end of third grade, I was bullied. This isn't an unusual experience by any means. It's reasonable to say that every student can recall a time when they didn't feel safe at their school. Bullying started for me because I wasn't willing to conform to a clique. Kids my age had certain archetypes they fit into: sports jocks, Dungeons and Dragons players, the popular kids, the geeks and nerds, band kids, and misfits. I wasn't drawn to any particular group, and so I spent a lot of time on my own.

One of the most humiliating things that happened came from a girl named Erica Fisher. During our PE period, we were escorted outside by our teacher to play a coed game of softball. Normally, I got along with Erica and her friend Elizabeth, but for some reason, I was their target that day. Elizabeth said, "Hey, Branden. I have a new nickname for you: GID. Girl in disguise." Erica laughed, took the baseball bat, and hit me right between my legs, and they both started laughing. I fell to the grass in agony and crawled along the side of the fence, coddling my manhood. The teacher didn't take notice, and not a single student came to my defense. Instead, the majority of the class started to laugh at me as tears of humiliation and pain streamed down my face.

I was trapped in school bathrooms and punched and poked in the stomach to the point of bruising—socked in the arm and given charley horses on my legs on a regular basis. I would avoid taking my shirt off at home in front of my mom and dad because I didn't want them to see what was going on. Just about everyone called me by my beloved nickname, Girl in Disguise, until I changed schools. I chose to spend the remainder of my lunches and recesses in the library because it was a safer place. On occasion, I would act out and ruin a classmate's assignment or be disruptive in class. I had to release all of my pent-up hurt and anger somewhere, after all.

As an adolescent, I was a master at self-monitoring, and that little voice we all have in our heads constantly reminded me of my shortcomings. I turned to music during these dark times. My parents must've picked up on my energy, because it was about this time they spent their last $500 to buy me a secondhand piano. The morning my parents decided to buy a piano, my dad was racing around the house proclaiming, "We are going to buy a piano for Bub today, and God is going to figure out a way for us to pay for it." Sure enough, by late that afternoon, after scouring through the local newspaper classifieds, we came home with a walnut-brown Baldwin studio piano that had been on display at a garage sale. The people who sold it to us gathered their helpful neighbors and hoisted it into the back of my brother Jason's vintage El Camino. I was so excited about my new toy; I jumped in the back of the flat-bed car and played the out-of-tune piano all the way home.

My mom quickly organized a piano tuner so I could practice with all eighty-eight keys in sync. I had been studying on a keyboard for about four years at that point, but this was the first time I had anything with more than four octaves available to me. My piano became my friend—I could safely leave all of my secrets on its keys. I felt whole and authentic when I played the piano, and to this day, I am most comfortable on stage when I'm playing it and singing. My connection to the piano has a spiritual nature. I worship it, in a sense. No form of therapy could have been more effective for me during those turbulent years.

This gift of my first piano, however, wasn't some great catalyst for a renewed drive to practice my assigned repertoire. Throughout those short years of formal study, my teachers kept leaving me because I wouldn't practice. I preferred to play music by ear rather than follow a traditional tutelage. I learned Beethoven's "Für Elise" by ear, played a small, red, five-hundred-page worship song fake book from cover to cover, and played many a Disney song instead of running through the typical development courses assigned to me by my teachers.

Mrs. Johnson, my very first piano teacher in Anaheim, used to take the lead end of her pencil and jab my hand every time I made a mistake. I would take my small Casio keyboard over to her house on Tuesdays after school to endure this torture. Today, this would be considered assault or abuse by some parents. I was lucky to avoid her prodding for the most part in the beginning, but when the music became more difficult and I started making mistakes, I'd leave my lessons with black marks and welts all over the tops of my hands. I never told my parents because I thought it was normal. At the time, it probably was.

My second piano teacher was Alice Moretti, our family piano tuner and another mentor of sorts. She told my parents that I had perfect pitch and should learn to sing someday. I won a couple of piano competitions under her direction—playing all three movements of Beethoven's *Moonlight* Sonata and mastering the Bach Inventions. I had a statue head of

Beethoven to prove my winnings. My brothers quickly translated the figurehead into a nickname and would scream at me, "Shut up, Beethoven!" if they could hear me banging away over their beloved football games from the family room. I never took it as an insult. I just thought how stupid they were, since Beethoven was a bona fide genius.

Eventually, Ms. Moretti, personal piano tuner to Bruce Hornsby at the time, figured out her commute wasn't worth my lax attitude toward practicing what she assigned me. So she left. My third and final piano teacher was an attractive, very well-groomed blond man in his thirties. I can't recall his name, but I do remember this: he just flat out said to my parents one day, "The money you're spending on Branden's piano lessons isn't worth it for you. He isn't practicing during the week, and this has become a waste of your time and mine." My parents had other mouths to feed, so they made a pragmatic decision to halt my weekly lessons.

While I should have hung my head in shame, I was instead relieved at the idea that I could keep playing piano just as I wanted to. I wasn't driven to get better, not ever. However, my piano skills did get me my first gig at a young age. When I was thirteen years old, I was invited to entertain on a weeknight at my grandma O'Connell's assisted-living home. I was offered twenty-five dollars as a payment. I remember getting in our luxury blue family van, complete with a VCR and television antenna to entertain us kids on long road trips. My stomach was filled with butterflies. Still, I managed to put on a forty-five-minute recital, which much of my extended family attended. I played every easy-listening hit you could imagine, from Barbra Streisand's "Evergreen" to "Memory" from *Cats*. My song choices alone would make someone's gaydar go ballistic, but I hardly even recognized it at the time.

I was far too shy to sing in public. This is something I would do after school in the garage before my parents would get home, or late at night on a weekend when my brother was out for the night. I would pull out tapes with tracks to songs by Milli Vanilli and Linda Ronstadt, from movie soundtracks such as *Beaches* and *The NeverEnding Story*, insert them into the machine, grab the mic, and sing my guts out. I still do this at home—generally in front of the piano, and now, luckily, with James as my accompanist.

At our family gatherings, it was always a mission of my mom's to make me play piano for the family. I visibly resisted and resented her every time she made the request. There were two major reasons I did this: first, I was terrified at the idea of performing in front of people, especially *those* people. I loved my relatives dearly, but my cousins were all much older or younger than me, and I was at that awkward age when none of them wanted to play with me. Instead, I just seemed to naturally gravitate toward my aunts and my grandmother. I was always most comfortable around the ladies. All the men and boys in the house were watching college football and discussing sports. I just couldn't relate, so I spent time helping out the girls and my mom in the kitchen.

The second reason I didn't want to play the piano was that my biggest fear was being vulnerable in front of people. Performing music exposes a piece of your soul, and since my modus operandi at the time was to hide everything that was transparent about me, this put me in a precarious position. Even now, years later, I get nervous and sweaty when I perform in front of small groups of people: say, in someone's living room. Or when I'm asked to sing on an impromptu basis in public—I shudder at the thought of doing it. Forget about karaoke. I *hate* it. I'd rather sing the National Anthem at the Super Bowl. I suck at karaoke, and nothing makes me more anxious than waiting and wondering when my song might be called. Still, after much resistance, I would eventually cave and do as I was told: play the piano. Later on, when the family knew I was capable, I would also sing.

The inspiration for my parents buying me a portable karaoke machine came from what I refer to as my first recording. For the years my dad owned a distributorship, we were invited as a family to attend yearly sales conventions. These trips took us to places such as San Diego, Hawaii, and Nashville: all sophisticated destinations for a family whose travel had previously extended to Lake Shasta or the occasional weekend trip to Las Vegas to camp in the KOA campground. My parents took three of us to the convention headquarters at the Grand Ole Opry hotel in Nashville one year, to experience the South and have a bit of a family vacation. In our hotel room, I would move toward the balcony and wrap myself in the curtains, hiding myself to the public, and sing at the top of my lungs. Small crowds would gather below and clap and wonder who the mystery kid singer was.

We spent a day at Dolly Parton's theme park, Dollywood, on that vacation. Ms. Parton had some recording booths set up in the park where you could pay a hefty fee, pick a song, go into a recording studio, and come out with a testament of your own singing skills. My brother Shane chose the Ben E. King classic "Stand by Me." He sang it with so much heart but just couldn't carry a tune to save his life. My dad predictably chose an Elvis Presley song, and having country music in his blood, delivered a one-take performance with convincing tone and nuance.

Next it was my turn. I chose "Wind Beneath My Wings" from *Beaches*. Though rough around the edges, I gave a passionate and very melodic performance that shocked my family. I recently listened to that tape recording and was impressed with my skills at ten years old. My karaoke machine functioned just the same as my yellow record player and my piano. For a solitary kid, they were all my friends. I knew I enjoyed singing, but I didn't know I was actually any good at it—yet.

CHAPTER
THREE

I n these confusing times, I slowly figured out my identity but still kept it a secret from everyone. Church was
the center of my life, whether I wanted it to be or not. I
remember having some disagreements with my dad about
going to church on Sunday mornings. He told me, "As long
as you're under my roof, you'll go to youth group every week
and you'll go to church every Sunday with your family."

It didn't stop there. I attended winter church camps in
Idyllwild, California, Christian music conferences with
friends in Estes Park, Colorado, worship nights with my
youth group at Zuma Beach, and church potlucks at our
community church. I'd also attend men's-only conferences
with my dad and brothers, called Promise Keepers. These
conferences would last an entire weekend, and the events
were a combination of church and male bonding in a huge
stadium. The leaders of the conference would discuss the
gravity of saving oneself for marriage, dedication to your
wife, and the importance of being an example of God to
your current or forthcoming family.

These concepts were nearly impossible for me to relate

to. I could comprehend them, of course, but could never find an authentic way to apply them to my life. I was gay. I didn't envision having a wife or children. I understood those things wouldn't be a part of my future in the traditional sense even before I was comfortable with my own sexuality. I just *knew* it wasn't in my time ahead.

Something I did connect with at these virile conferences was the emotion of the worship music. I'd hear just a few bars of Crystal Lewis singing "Come Just as You Are," and I would get sentimental and teary eyed. Music has a power to reach down into the very core of our beings. It was the *music* that pulled me closer to God. I have a vivid memory of standing with my two older brothers and my father, huddling in a circle, praying and crying together while we watched our tears cascade off the ends of our noses into a puddle on the stadium concrete. Thousands would gather for the altar call, and the sheer sight of all of these men committing their life to God could take anyone's breath away. With thousands gathered together, we fed off each other's emotions. Even though I wasn't buying most of the doctrine, the experience still profoundly affected me.

In high school, I also attended youth group summer camps. At one such camp, I remember sleeping in bunk beds in a large room with twelve other boys and our youth group leader, Dustin. It felt to me like there was a lot of sexual tension in the room. One of the boys would parade around the room without any clothes on, bearing an erection, and our leader, Dustin, would pick up a broom and say, "Put that thing away." I remember some of the group conversations we shared those nights, before we all fell asleep. I told them all a story about what I believed to be a ghost that would come out at night and stand at the foot of my bed. I claimed that it was always there, watching over me while I slept. I went on to say that sometimes I'd walk through the shadow of the ghost to get to the bathroom, and it would be cold, almost freezing.

Of course, *none* of this was true, but lying was my way of getting the attention I needed. I lied to my parents about almost everything through my teenage years. They had no clue that I drank beer and liquor, smoked cigarettes occasionally, and experimented with marijuana. They didn't know who I was dating or where I'd been spending my time. I stuck to one golden rule to make my parents trust me: I always made sure to come home on time.

My brother Shane and I also once spent a few weeks at a sportscentric Christian summer camp called Supercharge at Westmont University. It was like a megachurch for kids, and we were taught everything from a heterosexual, evangelical perspective. Again, the spirituality of the music was the easiest part to grasp in this environment. I met a girl there from Bakersfield named Christina, who befriended me. She was a beautiful girl with a huge personality and long blond hair that extended down below her backside.

On one of the final nights of the camp, there was an organized dance with mandatory attendance. Christina and I were instant kindred spirits, despite the awkward romantic advances she made at me. How was she to know I was gay? And how was I to tell her without compromising myself? We slow-danced to "End of the Road" by Boyz II Men. She opened her mouth on one of the choruses, and I discovered that she was a legitimate singer whose voice possessed a beautiful quality I'd never heard before. My body was overcome with euphoria. She enchanted me like a siren. I pulled her closer to my ear so I could better hear the bewitching sounds. It was the first time I became aware of my passion for the live sound of the human voice and my desire to explore my own singing.

The summer before my junior year, my family moved to Irvine, California. I met a girl in youth group named Jasmine Bleecker. One early evening in August, shortly after I had obtained my driver's license, I was driving with Jasmine and playing the music of Amy Grant's Christmas album in our family van. I was singing along, making up a harmonized part, thinking I was being quiet. She heard me and said, "You know, you really should audition for the choir at school."

I thought, *What the hell? Why not?* I was at the age when I was meant to have some sort of plan for my collegiate future. My friends were talking about their big plans to get into the prelaw program at USC or to study medicine at UCI. I had absolutely no idea what I wanted to do with my life, nor where I wanted to go to school. My plan at that point with my unbalanced grades was to go to community college and hope that some interest kicked in. When I was a kid, I used to take those aptitude tests to see what my vocation might be. I scored highest as a potential dental hygienist or flight attendant. I would have been happy with one of those, I guess: I would have gotten to travel to amazing places and have a steady income. Then again, it could have meant a career of passing out snacks to people with nut allergies, or treating gingivitis.

The day came in late August when it was time to enroll in next year's classes at my high school. My mom took me up to the school and helped me start the process. I suggested I might want to enroll in the school chorus as an elective. My mom, always attentive to my wishes and supportive of my decisions, said, "Why not? It'd make your grandpa James very proud."

I discovered that upon enrolling, I had to schedule a private audition with the choral director, Mr. Bates. An audition? What was that? I could only equate it to tryouts in sports. I was afraid I would be completely out of my league. But from the moment I walked into the music building, which housed the school band, orchestra, piano lab, and choral department, I felt like I was at home. I was greeted by a friendly woman named Janelle Murphy, the school accompanist, who told me upon arrival, "Mr. Bates will be with you in a few moments. He's just finishing with another student."

I took a seat on the escalated choir rows of the rehearsal room. From my point of view, there were two green chalkboards and one whiteboard, on which sat an assortment of dry-erase markers and a shelf full of sheet music. There was a funny scent in the building that reminded me of old books you might smell in a library. Something about it was comforting. I sat fidgeting for a few more minutes until Mr. Bates and the student he was auditioning appeared from a tiny, triangle-shaped studio with a small, walnut-brown Yamaha piano inside.

He greeted me with a warm smile and said, "Branden, is it?" I nodded. "Come with me."

He proceeded to ask about my musical history and my experience with singing. They were easy questions to answer: "I'm an amateur pianist and have never sung in my life," I replied.

"Okay, not to worry," he said. "Let's start with some scales. Sing these notes back to me on the word, *la*. Like *fa, la, la,* and we'll go down from there."

I followed his instructions with some trepidation: I barely grasped what he said but was able to rely on my ears to follow him. We vocalized down to the bottom of my range, a low G. One thing I *could* do was read music and locate pitches on the piano. This was a great aid to me in the audition process. We started again at middle C and did the same scales, but ascended this time. He had me vocalize up to a high C.

When I finished, he said, "Wow. You have a phenomenal ear and an amazing range for a high school student. What did you bring to sing for me today?"

"Nothing. I didn't bring anything."

"That's okay," he said. "Would you prefer to sing 'Happy Birthday' or perhaps 'My Country 'Tis of Thee'?" I chose the latter one. We got through the first verse and chorus of the American standard, and then he stopped.

"Branden, have you really never had any formal vocal training?"

"No," I replied, confused.

"That was probably the best audition I've ever heard from a high school student in my thirty years of teaching." I was blushing, and I didn't have any clue what to say. He asked more questions. "What is your schedule like this year? Are you playing any sports, or are you committed to any other activities?"

I said, "No. I'm done with all of that, I think."

He kept going with his giant Cheshire cat grin: "I would like to put you in the high school chorale, and also the Irvine

Singers, which is both a chamber choir and a show choir for advanced singers. Do you think you could make time for both programs? We could really use a voice like yours."

I went silent for a few seconds, deliberating whether or not I was brave enough to suddenly become a singer. "Let me talk to my parents about it, but I think so, yes."

"Excellent," he replied. "Now how old are you?"

"I'm sixteen years old."

He jumped off the piano bench with childlike excitement. "Great, let me go and get you some music. Janelle, could you please come to the piano?" Janelle scurried toward the piano and was handed a piece of sheet music called "What I Did for Love." I was given the same music, and Mr. Bates had a copy as well. He said, "We're going to try something called sight singing. Since you play piano, I don't think this will be too difficult for you. Using your voice, can you read the tenor line on page three, please? It's a simple concept: when the notes go down, your pitch goes down. When the notes go up, your pitch goes up. The rhythms are held for the same note value that you would play on the piano. Janelle will help you by playing your harmony line with you."

I proceeded to sing "What I Did For Love" but spent a couple of minutes making mistakes.

Mr. Bates finally stopped me. "Don't worry. You'll get the hang of it," he assured me. "Thanks for coming in today. Go and speak to your parents about this, and we'll see what happens."

I was ushered out the same back door as the previous student, and I left in shock, looking blankly for my mom's vehicle in the sea of cars in the parking lot. I finally spotted her and got in the car without a word. She put it into reverse and asked, "Well. How did it go?"

"Good, I think," I said. "He wants me to be in two different choirs. One regular choir and one advanced, smaller chamber choir."

"Branden! That's amazing news! Good job!" said my mom enthusiastically. There was just a week left before school started, and suddenly I had something to look forward to. *Could I actually sing? Or was there some other reason this new opportunity was in front of me?* I was doubtful but willing to give it a shot.

School commenced shortly after Labor Day—my first day at a new school, with no friends. I got through my first three periods: political science, geometry, and English. It was all so overwhelming, and a bit embarrassing not knowing anyone. Fourth period arrived, and it was time for chorale. I'm not sure if I was more frightened or excited. I walked into the classroom and nearly everyone stared at me. Finally, I saw a familiar face in Jasmine Bleecker. Many of the kids were talking with each other as if they'd known one another for years. Mr. Bates greeted me and said, "Hello, Branden. Welcome. Please go and sit with the tenors."

He gestured just up and to his left, and I found a chair, picking up the tattered navy-blue leather choir folder from my seat and planting myself next to a clan of other awkward teenagers. A brace-faced, curly brown-haired guy with a friendly smile poked my back from behind and said, "Hi. I'm Barry."

Sweat was dripping down the small of my back. "Hi. I'm Branden." I cowered back into my seat and shuffled through my music as if I had something important to do.

Barry spoke up again, "Don't be scared. We're all friendly here." I just gave him a half smile in return and looked back down at my materials.

A sterile bell rang, and class commenced. Mr. Bates welcomed all of the students. "Let's go straight into a group warmup," he said.

We started buzzing our lips, trilling our tongues, taking large, low-breathed inhalations, and exhaling as slowly as possible. We sang through scales of the five Italian vowels of ah, eh, ee, oh, and oo. All of it was foreign to me, but I felt comforted knowing that I had the support system of fifty-nine other voices who were asked to do the same thing.

After we warmed up, Mr. Bates said in his Iowan dialect, "All righty, let's go ahead and break the ice. Shall we?"

I wasn't sure what he meant, but the accompanist, Janelle, started right into the intro of "My Country 'Tis of Thee." And sure enough, there were the lyrics to the song on the chalkboard in front of us. Mr. Bates spoke over the top of the music, giving us some simple instructions. "We'll start on the top row and go across the room to the end of the row, and then continue on to the next row, etc. Amy, is it? On the top left? We'll start with you. Sing the first half of the verse and then, Jenny, you sing the second half, and so on. Does anyone have questions?" He squinted his eyes and scanned the room for raised hands. "No questions? Go ahead, Amy," he commanded.

Amy waited for the intro loop that had been playing to come back to the entrance point and then proceeded to sing. A small, mousy soprano voice came out of her, which was shaky, as she was visibly nervous. Next, Jenny rang out with a bellow of confidence but didn't quite hit the pitch.

Land where my fathers died, land of the pilgrims' pride. From every mountainside, let freedom ring.

As the sing-off progressed, with each person warbling down the rows, I started to do the math to figure out which lyrics I would be singing. I deduced that I would get the "land where my fathers died" lyrics, which I was happy with. My stomach rumbled and sank with rapid intensity as the song inevitably approached me. I stopped to listen to the friendly, handsome boy Barry, who had earlier said hello to me. *Nice voice*, I thought. And just like that, the slight, red-haired kid sitting to my left chimed in with a vibrato that sounded like a jackhammer. *Oh shit. It's my turn. Here we go.* I focused on the chalkboard and started in, at first nervously and eventually with more confidence until my assignment was over. Several girls let out audible "woos" and even a quiet clap as the intro music started again for the next singer.

After the exercise was over, there was a much lighter energy in the room. We moved on to cover the expectations of the curriculum, grades, attendance, rehearsal, and memorization deadlines for specific pieces of music. Mr. Bates announced the dates for the fall concert. On the dot of 11:40, the school lunch bell rang, and Mr. Bates said, "Great work, everyone. We'll see you tomorrow. Don't forget to speak to your parents about the open positions on the IHS chorale boosters board."

Since lunch was the next activity, some students pulled out homemade meals from their backpacks and socialized in their seats. A small crowd of students gathered around me to introduce themselves and compliment me on how beautiful my voice was. I didn't know what to say. This was all new to me—I'd never received compliments like this. A few of the girls introduced themselves to me. "Hi, I'm Amy," said one girl. "Hello, I'm Monica," said another girl.

I shook their hands and said, "Nice to meet you." They blushed and giggled their way out of the rehearsal room.

Mr. Bates walked over and asked me if he could speak with me for a moment in his office. I obliged and followed him, nervous about the whole thing. In just one class session, I'd been able to assess his personality, and I already understood clearly that he could stoke fear in any one of us without notice. The first day of class didn't keep him from holding back his no-bullshit sort of character. He grew red in the face and impatient when we weren't holding the shape of the pure vowels he'd previously demonstrated. He blew up at a disorderly student and told him to choose a different elective if he planned to continue to disrupt his class. He embodied intimidation despite his friendly, Midwestern, sometimes folksy tone.

Mr. Bates welcomed me into his tiny office decorated with plaques from wins at choral competitions over the years. There was a bookcase behind his desk filled with musicology books, opera scores, art song anthologies, and some unrelated titles as well. Just above the bookcase were his undergraduate and graduate degrees, hung like a shrine on the wall. The commercial-carpeted floor had a small Persian rug on it, and he sat in a black leather office chair. On the wall just to the left of his chair was a small mirror intentionally placed for him to examine his appearance and fix his carefully styled, thick coiffure from time to time.

"Branden." He addressed me in his bass-baritone voice. "I can't tell you enough how impressed I am with your singing ability. I have a question for you. We're looking for new members of our board. Would your parents be interested in joining the chorale boosters board here in our department?" I replied with a very long story, explaining that my father was on disability and my mom worked two jobs. I told him that I didn't think they would have the time or money to be involved, but I would speak to them about it.

"Oh, I'm sorry to hear all of that. Not to worry. I completely understand. I have one more thing," he said, and he pushed a photocopy of some sheet music toward me. "We have a fall concert coming up, as I mentioned in class, and I would like you to sing a solo. How would you feel about that?"

I glanced down at what he'd slid in my direction. It was a piece of music called "Beautiful Dreamer," written by Stephen Foster. I recognized the name of the composer, but I had no idea from where.

Mr. Bates told me, "Go home and play through it on the piano, and have a sing through and see what you think. You can let me know next week if you'd like to perform it at the concert." He raised his left eyebrow as if to tell me that I didn't have a choice. "Ah! One more question, I almost forgot. Would you be interested in enrolling in drama class?" He peered down at some notes he had sitting in front of him. "I see in your schedule you have space for one more elective, and I think it would be great for you. I can introduce you to Mr. Green, the drama teacher, if you'd like."

I paused for a moment and then said, "Sure," with a perplexed smile. This was clearly going to be the year of trying new things.

"Okay," he said, smiling at me. "Sorry to have cut into your lunchtime. We will see you tomorrow."

I left his office, grabbed my backpack, and tore out of the building with a grin on my face and a rush of enthusiasm. I headed for the quad—an outdoor amphitheater where many students chose to eat lunch—took out my brown paper lunch sack, and bit into my bologna sandwich. Only then did I let everything sink in. I was sipping on my Capri Sun and peeling my orange when I had an epiphany. I had a secret weapon: *my voice*. No teacher or group of students had ever treated me like that before. They all thought *I* was talented. How bizarre the whole experience was. Through coincidence, divine guidance, and cosmic timing, I believe this was the moment that music found me…and saved me.

CHAPTER
FOUR

t wasn't long until my identity as a singer manifested itself in my entire being. It was my calling. It became my addiction as well: the only thing that truly invigorated me. It made me a better version of myself—maybe even the *best* version of myself. From the moment I debuted as a singer at my high school concert and saw the teary eyes in the audience and the rush of people who came up to me afterward, I realized that I had something powerful inside me. My voice seemed to move people, to touch them at their core. My mom used to always tell me, "That voice of yours is a gift from the Lord. Don't forget to always use it for His glory." I discovered that I had a profound power that could actually change people. The only thing standing in its way was me. I still had my damaged self-esteem to contend with.

I was a much more dedicated vocal apprentice than I had been a piano student. It was a pleasure to practice and learn the art songs of Ralph Vaughan Williams and Roger Quilter, the standard arias of Mozart and Verdi, all the while expanding my musical theater repertoire and learning some songs that I just plain loved. At the same time, I was cast as Nicely-Nicely Johnson in the school production of the Lerner and Loewe musical *Guys and Dolls*. It was a bit of a stretch for me—literally. The character Nicely-Nicely is traditionally an overweight alcoholic. Although I was merely a scrawny teenager, I could still rock a seersucker suit. The drama teacher made an exception and cast me in the role, which only confirmed my snap decision to give up recreational sports for music. Eventually, I was awarded my pick of most any solo at the many concerts our choirs gave.

Doing all of this with hardly any real confidence was a difficult endeavor. I was so uncomfortable in my body that I couldn't move or act or dance, let alone walk and sing at the same time. I had to have special coaching sessions with the assistant drama teachers on how to deliver a song, deliver dialogue, and play a character. I spent extra hours in choreography lessons simply learning to step-touch.

Because of this obvious lack of training and the flaws in my confidence, the favor I received from my choral and drama teachers didn't go over well among the other boys in our classes. They probably didn't understand why I was given all of these opportunities with so little performance talent. While I formed friendships (primarily with the three other boys I sang in a barbershop quartet with), there was quite a bit of disdain and jealousy lurking about. During an orchestra dress rehearsal—the crucial rehearsal, sometimes referred to as a *Sitzprobe* or *Wandelprobe*, where the singers get to rehearse with the orchestra a few times before the opening performance—for *Guys and Dolls*, I walked back to the dressing room after the opening sequence of the show. The door was cracked open just enough for me to see the reflection in the mirror of one of the guys from the ensemble. In front of a crowd of other guys, he was mocking me, imitating me in a throaty, operatic tone.

Instead of singing the written lyrics "Can do, can do…" he sang, "Can't act, can't act, this guy shouldn't sing, can't act." I ran away as fast as I could so the others didn't know I had overheard them. Needless to say, I didn't spend much time in the dressing room for the rest of the run. High schoolers were vicious. Kids are just mean to each other, full stop. I suppose the same can be said for some humans in general.

Even so, I felt like I was liberated by spending my last two years of high school in Orange County versus my first two years in Newbury Park. Aside from the newfound confidence and musical identity I experienced, there seemed to be other gay guys at this school. Of course, none of us talked about it with each other, but it was evident at the slightest glance. There was so much subtext in a simple gaze. To this day, I can look another gay man in the eye and tell immediately that we are of the same sexual preference.

But I dated girls throughout high school. My first girlfriend was Kendra, who also lived in Newbury Park. She was a beautiful, blonde Christian girl whom I had met in youth group. She had crystal-blue, almond-shaped eyes and gorgeous long hair. Kendra was wise beyond her years, and we had a true friendship and connection. We used to spend a lot of time together at the piano playing through worship songs at her house or mine. Her mother, who called herself Tippy, suffered from constant migraines and confined herself mostly to her room—however, she'd emerge every once in a while to show us lyrics to a song she wrote. Kendra and I dated for three and half years and referred to each other as our first loves. Our relationship lasted even through my family move to Irvine.

Apart from the four school dances I spent with Kendra, I attended fifteen prom and homecoming dances in my four years in high school. I just couldn't say no, I suppose. It's not that I was having a ridiculous amount of fun—it's more that I just felt obligated to say yes to these strong-willed girls who asked me to be their date on their first real Cinderella evening. I traveled far and wide around Southern California to attend other schools' dances, and my escort services were paid for by many a girl's parents. Gay men are a dream at first sight for many girls. We're sensitive to their needs and in touch with our own emotions. We don't mind going shopping with them, gossiping, or watching romantic comedies. It was always easy to treat girls with politeness and dignity while respecting their personal boundaries. I've always bonded with women and cherished them. Aside from the kinship my husband and I share, my closest and longest-lasting friendships are with the powerful women whom fate just plopped down in my life for one reason or another.

Over those last two years of high school, I dated several girls and explored sexual endeavors, discovered marijuana, and continued to drink on occasion at school parties. The other kids were doing it, and since I was becoming more comfortable there, having been branded a hero in my music department, I joined in. All of this was kept under wraps from my parents. There *was* one occasion where my mom dropped me off at church on a Sunday morning and asked me, "Branden, do I smell alcohol on your breath?"

I flat out lied and said, "No, that must be my mouthwash you're smelling."

I'm not sure if she believed me or not, because she never said anything more. As a parent, I'm sure you have to pick and choose your battles wisely.

Then there was the time I went to my senior prom, when some of us had arranged to rent a hotel room on Balboa Island. I knew that if I'd asked permission, my parents would never have granted it. So instead, I made up a fake story about sleeping over at my friend Barry's house, and they bought it.

That night, they let me take the red convertible Ford Mustang to drive my date to the dance and beyond. We had a wonderful evening at the dance and then later threw a party at the hotel that came with an arsenal of alcohol. When I parked the car at the time, I didn't take note of the restrictions, and I woke up the next day with a parking ticket to accompany my hangover. Since I didn't have the money to do anything about it, I ripped the ticket up and threw it away.

I wasn't always the most sensible kid: I could have easily asked my friends to put in some money and paid it on the sly. Instead, a notice arrived in the mail about six weeks later addressed to my father, whose name the car was registered in. It didn't take my parents long to discover what had happened and my whereabouts that night. I was grounded for lying to them and had to use my earnings from my part-time job at Knowlwood to pay for the ticket.

Teenagers make a melodrama out of everything, and I was no different. At one point in high school, I was dating a beautiful girl with bright eyes who stood just about an inch shorter than me. I believed she was way out of my league, but she must've been infatuated with my singing, as many girls were. I lost my virginity to her in a spur-of-the-moment decision at her dad's place.

Around this same time, in this crucial, transformational period known as young adulthood, I had discovered the importance of journaling. My leather-bound brown diary was about the only place I could keep my most precious secrets. I never had any filter when it came to writing in my diary. Why would I? It was *my* diary. More than that, it was the only entity, other than God, that I could trust to allow me to shed all of my burdens without judgment. After my first full-fledged sexual experience, I wrote explicitly and furiously about the event in the diary.

Fast-forward a few days: I came home late one evening, and my dad was sitting on the couch waiting for me. My heart sank when I walked through the front door. He only did this sort of thing when we were late getting home or there was some bad news to relay. He swiftly called out my name when I walked through the door. All the lights in the house were turned off, and I could only make out portions of his face with the help of the streetlight that was seeping through our white wooden shutters. His face looked spooky and mangled, as if he were sitting around a campfire and had shone a flashlight on it to tell a spine-chilling ghost story, which only confirmed my fear that I was in trouble. He motioned for me to sit down.

"Branden. Your mom read something you wrote down that really disappointed her. She's in our room lying down, and she's very upset about it. You need to go and speak to her."

I tried to swallow the lump in my throat. "Okay," I said with some dismay.

Surprisingly, there was no chastising, reprimanding, or scolding from my dad—only a stoic invitation to go and see my mom. I slowly got up from the couch, went into the kitchen to drink a glass of water, and then passed my sister's room. I peered in and saw her sleeping soundly like a princess in her resting chambers. The next stop was a quick trip to the bathroom before my sentencing. I was dragging out the inevitable for as long as possible. I slowly washed my hands and thought about why my mother needed to speak with me at this hour on a Saturday night. I made a left out of the bathroom and slunk down the hallway to her room. It felt more like I was entering a dungeon.

The door was slightly cracked, and I gently knocked as I pushed it open and approached my mom. She was sitting up in bed, reading a devotional book and jotting down some notes. Her room was dimly lit by the bedside lamp. She removed her reading glasses from her nose and glared up at me, distress on her face. Scanning me as if she were some sort of human polygraph, she said, "Your sister was playing in your room and found your diary. She read about what happened with you and that girl the other night."

I burst into tears and fell over myself, straight onto her Berber-carpeted floor. "I'm so sorry, Mom. I didn't mean to disappoint you. I'm so sorry."

"Well, Branden, we are very disappointed in you," she lambasted. "God asks us to save ourselves for marriage. Not to mention this is just reckless behavior." She started crying, which only made me cry harder. In due course, we released all of the tears we had stored at that moment. Finally she admonished, "Your dad and I will have to punish you for this. Now go to your room. It's time for you to go to sleep."

I scurried out of her room and heaved like a panicked animal in the wild. I'd committed a major sin in the eyes of my parents, my church, and my God. I didn't know how I'd ever recover.

I lay awake all night that night, wondering what my fate would be and mourning over my loss of innocence in the eyes of my mom. I was heartbroken from my own behavior. As the night turned into the early hours of the morning, I replayed the story over and over again in my head. *Ashley is only nine years old*, I thought. *Did she truly happen to find my diary and stumble upon a page that had the word* sex *on it? And recognized it? And then proceeded to take it to my mom and show her?* The whole scenario seemed pretty unlikely the more I thought about it. I didn't believe my mom. I believed she'd lied to me and betrayed my trust by snooping in my room. A slow burn enveloped my body, and my guilt and shame slowly turned to anger. It was the first time as a young adult that I'd experienced betrayal. And it wasn't just betrayal from anyone—it was betrayal from my mother.

The time was fast approaching when I needed to think about a secondary education. My uncle Ted, my mom's oldest brother, was instrumental in helping me see the importance of going to college. My parents had never been to college, having been married with children by the age of twenty, so they weren't well equipped to provide this sort of guidance. My uncle became a true friend, a mentor, and a father figure to me, and remains so today. We have shared many meals together, particularly California-style Mexican food.

We bonded over our love for food and music. He would regale me with stories about his own struggles in life. As we discussed my ambitions, he would sketch out graphs for me and ask me thought-provoking questions. "What would be your dream career path? Are you thinking music might be the answer for you?"

Ted took me under his wing in the way I needed most at the time. Aside from sympathizing with my parents' financial and medical problems, he picked up on the idea that I was different. I'm sure he could see that I was gay. He was eventually the first family member I came out to, and we shared a long, emotionally charged conversation about it. He confided in me about friends of his that were gay and even some distant cousins of his and mine. But the most affirming piece of counsel came at the end of our talk. He told me, "Branden, I want you to know something very important, so listen up. And I speak for my entire family when I say this: your aunt Marion and I, and your cousins, are all fine with your lifestyle choices and sexuality, and we do not love you any less or any differently than we ever have. Understand?"

It was at that moment that I could see that maybe there was some light at the end of this tunnel. Maybe others in our extra-large, tight-knit, Latin Catholic family might accept me, and perhaps some *would* see the real me, as my uncle did.

My uncle Ted never had a son. I think he always craved the chance to bring one up, so I was his perfect subject. Our meetings became more frequent: so much so that at times, I'd spend more time with him than I would with my own parents. This never pleased my mom, but she allowed it to happen. He would take me to bookstores and research music schools with me. He never once doubted that I should pursue what I loved. Neither did my father. My dad always reminded me of that phrase "If you love what you do, you'll never work another day in your life."

One week during my senior year, my uncle Ted scooped up my dad and me and took us on a coastal California college tour. We visited schools in Northern California and explored their music programs: Chico State University, UC Santa Barbara, Cal State Fullerton, UC Davis, Sacramento State University, and the San Francisco Conservatory of Music. Ted was a major proponent of getting me out of Southern California. He believed it was important and necessary, even, to allow a child to spread their wings and have an opportunity to figure things out on their own. My mom had a different style of parenting—she wanted us under her watch at all times. She preferred that we'd never leave the nest. I think her kids were one of her only respites from her unexpected life.

The day we stopped by the San Francisco Conservatory of Music was the day music would truly become my identity. After having failed at following the Thomas Guide map book for a while, we eventually found the school on Nineteenth Avenue and Ortega Street in the city limits. I knew from the moment I walked through the halls that I was home. Each room lining the stark hospital-like corridors had beautiful music wafting out of its doors: French horn, violin, piano, clarinet, harp, singing, flute, oboe, cello. It was a cacophony of chaos, but it was the most beautiful thing I had ever heard.

My uncle was a sales genius who most likely could sell ice to Eskimos if he needed to. Without hesitation, he waltzed into the admissions office, introduced himself, and convinced the administrative team to let me audition without going through any of the proper channels. They told us what the audition requirements were and asked if I was available in three days' time. Before I had a chance to speak, my uncle chimed in, "Yes. Of course. We'll be ready. Thank you very much." The three of us ambled around the school a little bit more and then sped off north toward Sacramento and Chico, California. While some of the campuses were impressive, and the vocal faculties were keen on my skills, I couldn't focus on any place other than the San Francisco Conservatory of Music.

We returned to the city the afternoon before the audition and checked into a hotel just off Union Square in San Francisco. While my dad and I were waiting for my uncle to finish checking us in, I came across a very thin woman on the street corner who was scantily clad and wearing heavy makeup. She approached me and said, "Excuse me, young man. I'm sorry to bother you, but I have no money and no place to sleep tonight. Is there anything you can help me with?"

I went charging toward my dad just as my uncle Ted came out. "Guys, that lady over there has no money for food and nowhere to sleep. We need to help her." My naïveté made my uncle and my father chuckle to themselves, all the while glancing in said lady's direction to make sure she wasn't paying attention.

"Branden," my uncle said, "I think that lady has a different agenda."

"What do you mean?" I asked with more urgency.

My dad replied this time. "Come here," he said, and he

pulled me close. He spoke softly in my ear. "Branden, that woman is a prostitute."

I had no idea. My gullible ways have been well documented since childhood.

The morning of my audition, my uncle took me to Macy's to buy a brand-new suit and shoes so I could appear at my best. It just so turned out I was prepared with the appropriate materials for the audition, and I passed with flying colors. I sang "O del mio dolce ardor" by Christoph Von Gluck and "Love's Philosophy" by Roger Quilter. The adjudication panel was impressed with my voice and my piano skills as well. They awarded me a hefty scholarship on the spot, and without any hesitation, I accepted their admissions invitation. I was ready for the fall of 1996, when I would be studying to achieve my degree as a bachelor of music candidate.

CHAPTER
FIVE

sprinted through my senior year of high school with absolute gusto. I played a leading role in the school musical and was honored with the chance to sing the National Anthem at my high school graduation. Meanwhile, my attendance at Disneyland never let up. I even mistakenly attended with friends during Gay Days. This particular weekend at Disneyland was designated for LGBTQ people. While there with friends, I screamed in disgust, "What you're doing is wrong, you faggots!" at two men who walked by me holding hands on Main Street, USA. I didn't know any better. I was taught that homosexuality was wrong and I was meant to speak out against it. The irony of me saying something like that was completely lost on me at the time. Homophobia exists even in the gay community.

Around the same time, I auditioned and was invited to attend an all-state honor choir week. I was a perfect addition to both the all-male and mixed choruses, and I knew it. Having been awarded the male solos for our big weekend concert, my ego enjoyed the attention I received. Over the course of the five days we spent rehearsing, one of the singers decided to throw a hotel party. There were twenty or thirty of us that attended. One of the students had smuggled in a few bottles of liquor and some wine. When we went through that stash, we opened the minibar fridge and ate and drank every single thing out of it. Later that night, I brought a boy back into my hotel room. We messed around a bit, I think. I was too obliterated to remember any details, but I'm certain my assigned roommate heard everything.

I woke up the next day in an outright fog and could hardly produce a sound after that mélange of liquor I'd consumed. About forty minutes into rehearsal for Morten Lauridsen's "Dirait-on" from *Les Chansons des Roses*, one of the copresidents of the organization came in the room and made an announcement.

"We've received word that someone in the choir threw a party in their hotel room and alcohol was served and consumed. Could the following people please come with me?" I trembled. *I was at that party. If I get in trouble, I'll be stripped of my scholarships and everything will be taken away.* The towering, dark-haired woman listed off names in a deep, commanding tone, ending with, "and Branden James, please come with me."

A growing whisper from the remaining chorus of 120 high schoolers cascaded across the room as the ten of us slowly rose from our seats. I closed my navy-blue rehearsal folder and stood up with my shoulders hunched, my neck tucked in, and my eyes peering at the ground. I could feel the stares from those around me in the tenor section and hear chortling and snickering in the background. It was like a scene out of a Harry Potter film. *There were more than ten of us there*, I thought. I must've been snitched on by someone else at the party. Or maybe by my disgruntled hotel room-mate?

We gathered up in the front of the auditorium, on dis-play in front of all the other singers, who were watching us like some sort of freak show. The stoic administrator led the pack into a light-filled corridor and up a flight of stairs to a long hallway with a row of chairs. At the end of the hallway was a double-doored entrance with two rectangular win-dows on each door. I could see the movement of adult fig-ures through the frosted glass. We all took a seat, and before we could blink, a man appeared and said, "Jamal Brown, right this way."

Jamal hopped out of his chair and dashed toward the man, and together they swept through the brown doors. Before his right leg had even made it through the entryway, the rest of us all looked at each other with terror in our eyes.

"What do we do?" asked one girl in a whispered panic.

"I don't know," said one of the boys. "But if my parents find out about this, I'll be kicked out of the house."

A girl with a pointy nose and square-framed glasses spoke up. "Listen! We don't have much time before he comes out of there. We all have to have the same story. We were in Jamal's room. We're not lying if we say it was him who threw the party. We can either say we weren't there, or we can say that we were there, but he had friends there and they ate and drank everything." My complexion was green. I was overheated and dehydrated from the nervous sweat that was dripping down my back.

Another boy spoke up. "We were there, but we didn't do anything. End of story. It was Jamal and his friends."

Everyone peered at one another with different shades of

guilt on their faces. Some audibly agreed to the trickery we were attempting to pull off, and the rest of us, who knew it was the only way to save ourselves, showed our acceptance in our expressions. I suddenly got a flash from the night before when I was drunkenly chowing down on crackers and an entire tub of whipped garlic-herb Boursin cheese.

We were called in one by one. Each of us gave the same whopper of a story to the committee of teachers, volunteer parents, and choral directors in the room. Out in the hall, each of us pretended to sympathize with Jamal while he sat there with us, worried over his fate. After the last of us came out of the room, a period of ten to fifteen minutes passed. Some of us turned the conversation to small talk, and others covered their faces in their hands and pressed their elbows against their knees in utter agony.

The man reappeared again and said, "Jamal, come with me." Jamal was an extremely slight boy who was wearing tight jeans, a denim shirt tied above his midriff, and enough eye makeup to rival RuPaul. Jamal was an easy target, and we all knew it.

After a while, he came out of the room with two of the adults and looked at each and every one of us with a stare of condemnation of our arrant betrayal. After he was escorted back down the stairs, we never saw Jamal again. I sit here still today and cannot believe what an asshole I was. How could I have allowed myself to blame the flamboyant gay guy for everything that had taken place? I was such a natural liar, having covered many times to protect myself for the better part of my life. Looking back on this behavior, I grieve for the person I was. Yet I also beam with pride when I realize how far I've come.

As a young person just realizing what his sexuality was, I wasn't yet aware of the alliances and protections I needed to put in place with others in the gay community. I was still a kid who knew no better than to watch out for himself. But knowing what I know now? Knowing how essential it is for my queer brothers and sisters to insulate one another? Knowing how much I betrayed a kid like me makes my heart ache. I persevered the rest of the weekend with a fake smile and a penetrating ache in my stomach. I sang my solos, took the applause and compliments, but left that weekend completely destroyed by no one but myself. I buried that story and have only shared it with one or two people until now. I am still ashamed beyond imagination.

There were just two months left before graduation. I had made a firm decision to go to the San Francisco Conservatory of Music. I wasn't offered free tuition, as I was at Cal State Fullerton, but something inside me knew I was meant to go north. Between searching for summer jobs, planning graduation, furiously rehearsing for school concerts, an event-filled social life, and studying hard to make sure I squeaked by in my algebra 2 class, I was one hundred percent engrossed in moving to San Francisco. It was only April, and my heart was already there.

The Corona del Mar baroque music festival was looking for another tenor, and Mr. Bates made sure I was a paid ringer. A ringer is a singer hired to fill in a gap that might exist in a section of a chorus or professional concert setting. I was a ringer through college at various churches from one end of the Bay Area to the other. I made this a source of income for many years in New York, Chicago, and Los Angeles, too. This was the second professional gig I'd been handed by my teacher. The first was at the Hollywood Bowl singing with the LA Master Chorale behind Florence Quivar in a concert version of *Aida*. I was only seventeen years old when I learned the triumphal march from Verdi's cherished opera.

I met a twenty-seven-year-old guy at one of these gigs, and he and I were transfixed by one another. As a closeted senior in high school, and someone who wasn't clever or devious enough to have my parents drop me off at one place and then go to another, we decided after our final performance at the festival to have a date of sorts at Disneyland. I didn't have a cell phone, but I daringly gave him our family phone line. Before the digital age, what other choice did I have but to accept his phone call and make plans? I knew that if I pretended that my girlfriend Melissa was calling and inviting me to the Magic Kingdom, it'd be easy to convince my parents to drop me off there. Turns out, we had an inconsequential day at Disneyland and I neither saw nor heard from him again. But it was a date, with a boy, while I was in high school, and neither my parents nor any of my friends had any idea. I was living a life that *no one* else knew about. And I wanted to live it more and more.

I was planning on performing a song with Sara Kopernik, a ballet dancer, friend, and fellow singer, at the senior concert. We decided that Billy Joel's "She's Always a Woman" would be a perfect song for me to sing while she did a solo dance on stage. Everything couldn't have ended better for me in high school. But all the while, I was in a state of remorse about Jamal and pondering what the end of *his* school year was like.

I got a job as a camp counselor for the summer, did a few

paid singing gigs here and there, continued to flip burgers, went on more dates with Melissa, and fixated on San Francisco. I only had a few pictures in my head of what San Francisco felt like: some views of the bay and city, the call girl on the street, the city sounds that seeped through the window while we'd slept with the windows open at our hotel, the Bashful Bull diner where I'd used their bathroom as a changing room and warmup studio, and of course the audition at the conservatory itself. But still, I couldn't help but fantasize about what my new life would be like.

I studied furiously at my vocal and piano skills and went to some summer parties. It was awkward returning to a high school party and making small talk with students who still had a year or two left before graduation. I'd moved on from that and didn't have any interest in hearing about next year. Consequently, all I wanted to do was talk about *my* next year, which I'm sure just thrilled the kids who were prisoners of high school for another twelve months.

I enjoyed the anticipation of these summer months, but it was also during this time that I experienced something that is unfortunately all too common in our society, especially in the entertainment industry. I had just turned eighteen that summer, and I was eager to move forward—with my music, my education, my relationships, my life. I was enthusiastic and innocent, and someone took advantage.

Suffice it to say, a man was passing through my area that summer who had tenuous ties to the music industry. He was only in town for a couple of days, but he heard me sing at one of my paid summer gigs and invited me to audition for him.

On a blisteringly hot summer afternoon in August, the man called and asked if I would come by his hotel for an audition, which he would tape. His stay in town was so short, he said, that he would only have time the following evening.

"Sure, that sounds great." Though I tried to play it cool, I remember thinking, *could this be my big break?*

The next night, my parents loaned me the family van. It had taken some effort to convince them to let me go on my own—but they had plans and weren't able to go with me that evening, and ultimately, they didn't want me to miss an opportunity. On the drive over to the hotel, I reflected on all of the amazing things that had transpired in the two years I lived in Orange County. Despite my dad's health issues and our family's continued financial problems, this place had served me well. I had a healthy college scholarship to look forward to, even with my just above-average grades and test scores. I was spreading my wings and leaving the nest to go study something I absolutely loved, and I had support all around me, from every corner of my universe. I'd never felt surer that I was making the best decision I could for my life: to study music.

I pulled our royal-blue monstrosity of a van into the hotel parking lot. I quickly found the room number he'd given me and knocked softly. The man opened the door and beamed when he saw me. He was dressed semicasually, in jeans and a collared shirt. I was most likely in a pair of tattered denim trousers myself, with a striped T-shirt and my wavy hair fanned out like Farrah Fawcett.

"Hello, Branden! Thanks so much for coming by." I crossed the threshold with the usual phony politeness that my friend Larry claims I put on when I enter anyone's place.

The man walked me over to a table in the corner, where he'd put out some bottles in a row, as if it were a bar: red and white wine and a few other minibottles from the hotel fridge.

"How would you feel about having a drink?"

I scanned my mind for a moment, knowing I had to drive home eventually. "I suppose I could have one," I said.

"What do you like?" he asked. I looked at him in bewilderment. I'd had drinks before, but it was generally a Keystone lager or a teenage concoction in a red Solo cup, or perhaps Boone's Farm Strawberry Hill straight out of the bottle. I didn't grow up in a family of drinkers. In fact, our house was completely dry. "Do you like sweet or dry?"

"What does dry mean?" I asked.

He peered at me with one eyebrow raised, as if the answer should be obvious.

I shook my head and said, "I don't know. Surprise me."

He settled on the red wine, handed me a glass, and raised his own to give a toast. "To finding new musical talent," he gushed. "It's not very often I hear a voice like yours."

I blushed a bit, took a sip, and my felt my face pucker in both curiosity and disgust. "Wow!"

He laughed and said, "I suppose it's an acquired taste." He also offered me some chocolate mousse that he'd ordered through room service. As anyone who knows me can attest, I live for food, second to nothing.

As I ate the dessert, he started asking me more about my musical training, and then about my life. Moving from one conversation to another, we transitioned from red wine to white wine, and then to the mini liquor bottles. His tone was quite warm and fatherly, and I was happy to sit and listen as he told me about the glamorous music business in Hollywood. My face had become bright red and my head was spinning a bit. He gestured toward the couch, and the small coffee table in front of it. "Come with me. I want to show you something."

I followed his lead and watched as the man sat on the couch. "You know, Branden, there are a lot of gay men in LA. Did you know that?"

My breath caught, and I fumbled my glass. *How did he know?* I hadn't uttered a word about my sexuality, of course. And I had no idea why he would bring it up now.

CHAPTER
SIX

mentioned earlier that I'm aware that I have good genes. There has always been a noticeable amount of staring from other gay men, and some women as well. Young kids stare in the same way, and it's obvious then, too, when we lock eyes, if we are of a similar orientation, even though the child may not yet know it. I've experienced this lingering gaze my entire adult life, and I know one day it will change, when I've aged some more. I suppose that's good motivation to aspire to stardom—hopefully at some point your fans don't mind how old you've gotten or how many face lifts you've had. Just wait and see, one day I'll be Tom Jones.

I've spoken to some older friends who say there comes a day when people simply stop noticing that you've even entered the room. My sixty-four-year-old Southern friend who speaks like he just jumped out of an episode of *Designing Women* regaled me one evening with stories over a drink: "I toured for years as a Chippendale, and now it's as if I'm not even there. Can you imagine? It's like I'm not even there!" he repeated a second time, even more resolute. Since I'm admittedly vain, being a performer and a public figure and all, I'm sure when this happens to me, I'll have a panic attack and make an appointment with the first plastic surgeon I can see. Ah! The quest for youth is doubly important in the life of a gay performing artist.

But despite being accustomed to attention, I was taken off guard by this stranger's question. What was so stunning about the confrontation was that it was the first time I had an adult engage with me on the subject of my sexuality. Only Melissa and I had spoken about it up to this point. I wasn't sure how to respond.

"Um, I don't know what to say."

"Don't worry about it," he assured me. "I understand."

I was stunned. We'd just finished talking about our families, and he'd mentioned an ex-wife. Was he telling me he knew *I* was gay? But then another question made my spine tingle.

"Have you ever had sex with a man?" *Why was he asking me about this?* He went on. "Because I have many times, and I quite enjoy it."

Silence. He was sitting on the sole couch in the room, so I sank slowly to the floor and sat on the carpet. It felt more like I was floating. My head was light, and I had a burning sensation running up the back of my shirt. I lowered my head for a few seconds and then heard his voice again.

"Branden?" He startled me. "It's okay. Just relax," he said.

I followed his gaze, and saw that he had taken out a magazine. He opened it, and I saw pornographic photos of young men inside. One of the photos depicted two men, and he pointed at it. "Do you think someday you might like to try this?" he asked.

Genuinely curious, and also unsure of what else to say, I asked him, "Does it hurt?"

"Yes. But it also feels good at the same time." He handed the magazine to me. "Take a look." There was more demand in his voice this time.

I fumbled through some of the pages, pretending to be interested in what I was seeing. But the truth was, I hadn't seen much pornography when I was growing up, so I didn't know what excited me. If my brothers kept it around the house, I sometimes found their stash. I would sometimes read my grandmother's romance novels or browse through suggestive magazines at bookstores. If I was lucky, I would catch the International Male catalog in the mail before my mom would throw it out. My parents had a copy of the film *Sliver* with Sharon Stone and Alec Baldwin hidden in a place they thought I wasn't aware of. Sometimes I would take out the VHS tape and watch the steamy scenes when no one else was home.

One can imagine the affront I felt when suddenly a stranger dumped pornography on me. It was sensory overload. The man would glance down at me every once in a while as I pretended to study the magazine. I was already so uncomfortable and frightened, I thought it'd be safest to put on a false front of enjoyment. He brought his glass of wine up to his mouth, took a sip, and asked, "How would you feel if I sat down and started gobbling on your cock?"

That repulsive question is something I will never forget. I immediately went into panic mode and stood straight up.

"I don't think so. That's not going to happen."

His friendly smile suddenly took on a possessed quality,

not unlike Jack Nicholson's smile in *The Shining*. "It's a lot of fun, you know. You'll enjoy it." The man was probably in his late fifties. I was just barely legal at eighteen. What in the hell was happening?

At this point, I knew that I had to leave as soon as I could. But if I didn't play it cool, I might not get out of there unscathed. A million realizations came flooding to my mind at once: *He must have never cared about my talent. I wonder if he's had interactions like this with other people.*

"Branden?" he insisted. "What do you think? Do you want to know what it feels like?" he pushed.

"Uh. I . . . um." I continued to rummage for the right words. "I don't think so. I don't want to."

"Come on." He continued to prod further.

He thinks I'm naive and stupid, but I know exactly what he's doing. He's trying to break me down. My subconscious was in full survival mode. I was like a Navy SEAL against a tide of manipulation, prepared for an epic battle of mind games.

"You know what, it's getting late, and I really should . . ."

Before I could finish the sentence, he blurted out, "You need to stay and wait for the alcohol to wear off."

Truth was, I should have waited to drive, but there was no way in hell I was staying another second with this man. I grabbed my light sweatshirt and darted toward the door. He cut me off at the entryway.

"Oh well. I guess I won't get to hear you sing," he said.

"Yeah," I replied. "That would be best." I helped myself to the door.

"All right. Thank you for coming over and for keeping this between us."

"Of course," I lied. He reached out as if to pat my shoulder, but at the last minute, pulled me toward him and put his wet tongue down my throat.

When his tongue made it past my lips, I recoiled and shouted, with more force than I had ever used before, "I need to go. Now!" He took the hint and released me.

"Goodbye, thanks again for coming." He slurred his speech while shoving the door shut.

I immediately jumped in the car, turned on the ignition, and pulled the gear shift into reverse as quickly as I could. My heart was racing. I was out of breath and beet red in the face—not to mention, well over the blood alcohol limit in California at the time. *Shit, shit, shit, shit, shit*, I said to myself over and over. What was I going to do?

The first thing I needed to worry about was driving home without hitting someone or getting pulled over. I stopped the car for one minute to catch my breath and make sure I could pull this off. If I got stopped by the police, my scholarship would be out the window, and I'd be going to community college.

About fifteen minutes later, I calmed down enough to just focus on the road and not on what had just happened. I turned right and took the back entrance to my parents' neighborhood; it was less visible and less likely to have cops lurking about. The front entrance to their neighborhood was right by the freeway, and it was common to see police cars gathering at the Denny's restaurant just opposite our street. I made it home safely and parked my parents' van in the driveway. I was thankful my parents were away that evening—I wasn't ready to face anyone yet, let alone allow my parents to discover how drunk I was.

I crept through our front door and ignored my usual

routines of getting a glass of water and brushing my teeth. I just went straight into my room, quietly shut my bedroom door behind me, buried my head in my pillows, and lay there processing everything. *He never thought I was talented; he was preying on me and leading me to believe that I was special. How did I not see it coming? Did he do this to others?*

Eventually, I passed out cold on my bed, still partially clothed. I'd had too many drinks over the course of the evening. I was awoken the next morning by the glaring sun coming through the miniblinds I'd left open the day before. My lips were crusted over from lack of hydration, my eyeballs were dry, and my hair was tousled from having slept facedown on my mattress. Shortly after I opened my eyes, my alarm went off. I could smell the stench of stale alcohol in the room, so I jumped up, opened the window, and turned on the fan in case one of my parents walked in. Memories of the night before crashed into my head, and I started to process everything that had happened. At that stage in my life, with hardly an ounce of confidence to stand on, I felt proud that I didn't allow him to rape me. I felt that's what would have happened if I had stayed.

I headed for the shower across the hall, passing my sister's room, where she played with her toys and talked to herself. I could hear the TV running the morning news in the family room and noticed the sweet smell of homemade cinnamon rolls wafting through the halls. I was extremely hungry for some reason—it must've been the hangover. I turned the shower on and stood on the mat, staring at the patterns on the bathroom wallpaper. The steam from the shower fogged up the bathroom and eventually roused me out of my stupor. I hurriedly jumped into the shower and let the hot water run over me. I felt dirty, violated. No amount of cleansing could wash away the shame and embarrassment that encased me.

Should I tell my parents? They'd never understand. My dad would go ballistic. Should I call the police? I'm eighteen. Is there anything they could do? Would they believe me, or would they even care? I had no clue what to do, so I decided that I would play it cool until I figured it out. I got out of the shower, dried my hair, threw on a baseball cap, some shorts, and a T-shirt, and tore down the stairs.

My mom greeted me as I walked past the kitchen. "Hi, Branden. Where are you off to? How was your audition? Would you like a cinnamon roll?"

She was an easy target to take my aggression out on. I snapped at her, "No, I don't need a cinnamon roll. The audition was fine, thanks. I have to go." I darted past her without giving her any of the things she deserved: a hug, a smile, an explanation. I kept walking for the door, hoping to avoid my dad, who was sitting in his reclining chair staring at the television.

"Hey, Bub," he endearingly called to me.

"Hi, Dad" was about all I could muster up in response, and I rushed out the door, leaving him with a perplexed look on his face.

I got back in the van, having forgotten to ask permission to use the car this time. I just had to get out of the house. I could only think about the force of the man's upper body pulling me toward him as I was trying to leave the night before, and the force of his tongue as it slipped into my mouth. Though still hot from the shower, I felt shivers down my spine, then sweat dripping down my scalp.

Since I can remember, I've always used food to absorb

my emotional pain, and this particular Saturday morning was no different. I went straight to my comfort zone: a local Mexican joint that we all ate at in high school because it was cheap and authentic. They were open every day for breakfast, so I knew I'd be in luck. I walked in and ordered two cheese enchiladas with rice and beans, a bean and cheese burrito, a beef taco, a side of guacamole, and a plate of nachos. I asked for extra chips and poured them out onto my tray, turning the tortilla chip boat into a giant container for the salsa bar. I sat down and ate every bite on my plate with intense fury. Wondering what in the hell I was going to do, I aimlessly cleared the drippings of my rage feast and scrambled back to the car.

On the drive home, I realized that I had only one option: to call my uncle Ted. He was the only person I could turn to. I couldn't tell my friends. It would be the biggest gossip in history. My parents would be so shell-shocked, they wouldn't know what to do. So I went home, put a smile on my face, and made small talk with my mom until I could grab the cordless phone, shut my bedroom door behind me, and call my uncle.

"Hi, Uncle Ted, it's Branden!"

"Well, hi, Branden!" he replied. "How are you today?"

"I'm not great, to be honest. Is there any chance you're free today? I really need someone to talk to."

He cleared his throat, his tone changing from jubilation to concern. "Yes, of course. I'm free anytime you need me. Where would you like to meet?"

"Is there any chance you can come to the Denny's by our house? I'll be on foot and need to meet you somewhere nearby."

"Of course," he responded. "Anything you need. I'm here to help." After arranging the details, I hung up the phone and just lay on the bed with my eyes open for a few minutes. My uncle lived about fifteen minutes south of us in Lake Forest. I knew I wouldn't be allowed to use the car any more that day, because my sister had soccer tournaments in the afternoon.

I walked into Denny's about five minutes before our meeting time. My uncle was already sitting at a table waiting for me with his day planner and a glass of iced tea. Sitting beside the glass were two empty packets of Sweet'N Low and a used spoon. I sat down and noticed him nervously scratching his right ear. It wasn't usual for me to call him and say *I need you.*

"What's going on?" he queried, continuing to itch his ear and blink his eyes more than usual. "You sounded pretty alarmed on the phone."

I waffled for a few seconds before I answered him. "I don't know. Well . . . nothing, really. Actually, something did happen, but I don't know how to talk about it." I lowered my head and paused for a while. "Uncle Ted, this is really hard." I kept starting and stopping sentences but didn't mutter anything that made sense.

"Is something going on at home?" he asked.

"No. Everything is fine there." I snapped at him a little bit. Bouts of unwarranted anger kept gushing out of me. This surprised him—it was completely out of character.

"Well, then, what is it?" he asked again, this time with more urgency.

I paused again, took a deep breath, and fearfully explained everything that had happened last night. I could see the rage building inside him; it was in his nature to be my protector. He listened intently, sometimes shaking his head in disbelief, and continued to play with his ear.

When I finished recalling everything, he nodded slowly. "Are you absolutely confident that everything you're telling me is the truth? No exaggerations here?" He begged for an accurate account.

"Yes. I'm absolutely sure," I said.

He was holding a heavy corporate pen, which he then proceeded to toss on the table in irritation.

"Branden, this is serious stuff you're talking about." He leaned toward me and lowered his voice. "Sexual assault? Serving alcohol to minors and then allowing you to drive home intoxicated? Man, oh man, Branden."

He put his hands over his face, rubbed his eyes a few times, raised his chin up in the air as if to look to God for an answer, and then shook his head briskly to clear away the wrath that threatened to consume him. It was the first time since the incident that I realized how serious the implications were. "Do your mom and dad know?" he asked.

I took a breath to answer him, but we were interrupted by a woman wearing all black with a name tag that read Shaylene. "Hello, there. Welcome to Denny's, young man. Can I get you gentlemen anything to eat?"

Still physically bloated from my Mexican binge, I decided to just get something to drink. "I'll have a chocolate malt with extra whipped cream," I said. I still had some more feelings to eat.

My uncle chimed in, "I'll have the Moons Over My Hammy sandwich and French fries, please. Can you make sure the fries are extra crispy? Thanks very much."

She said, "Okey dokey, I'll be back in a few minutes with your chocolate malt, sir."

When she said those words, my mouth salivated. I *needed* the comfort of that chocolate malt.

"No," I said, getting us right back into the conversation. "You're the first person I've told."

Ted opened his planner and jotted down a couple of notes. "Well, what do you think we should do about this?" he asked tenderly.

"I don't know. I have no idea."

"Well, I think we should go straight to the police, Branden. This isn't some game we're playing. We're talking about really awful things here. Laws have been broken. We have to do something about this."

I pondered the idea for a minute, and it sent me into a near panic.

"But what if people find out? What will they say?"

As a teenager, you're more worried about what other people think than what you think of yourself. I was concerned people wouldn't believe me. It's not like I had any proof.

"What are you thinking?" he asked.

"I, I, I think you're probably right," I agreed.

"I think your parents need to know before we go to the police."

I closed my eyes and exhaled a huge sigh, nodded in agreement, and then lowered my head. I opened my eyes after a few seconds, and the chocolate malt was sitting there, waiting to console me. I sucked it down in such a hurry that I got a brain freeze, and then moved straight on to the accompanying silver sidecar, spooning it into my mouth in record time.

"Are your parents at home now?" Ted asked.

"Yes," I replied. "For another hour, I think. They're leaving in a bit for my sister's soccer game."

"Well, let me get the bill and we'll head over there," he said, with his food only half-eaten. It was uncanny to see Ted leave food on a plate, so I knew he must've been overcome with worry.

We paid the bill and drove to my parents' house. I walked in, and my dad was vacuuming the house, as he often did on a Saturday. My mom was in her room, and my sister was in the backyard, fully dressed for her soccer game, playing with our dog and dribbling her ball around.

"Ted!" my dad greeted him. "It's nice to see you. What are you doing here?" Ted scanned the room for my mom.

"Is Lynda here?" he asked.

"Yeah, she's in the back."

"Branden and I have something we need to discuss with you both. Would you mind getting her, and maybe telling Ashley to stay outside for a little while?"

My dad was amenable to most every situation, except when it came to eating onions or blueberries—he has always had quirky food aversions. My mom came around the corner of the hallway as my dad instructed Ashley to stay outside for a little while.

"Hi, Lynda," Uncle Ted greeted her, with the kind of big hug that you give your youngest sister. "Branden and I need to discuss something with you."

My mom was clearly wondering why *he* knew about this discussion before she did. We all went into the living room. My dad sat on his reclining chair, Ted and my mom took a seat on the blue floral-print couch, just below her Marty Bell painting, and I sat in the primrose-yellow family heirloom rocking chair that my mom inherited from my great-grandmother.

Uncle Ted did all the talking. I just sat there, leaning forward on the chair with my elbows on my knees, staring blankly at the floor. I couldn't bear to see my parents' faces while he was talking. I became lost in my own thoughts until I was jolted out of them.

"What a sick jerk! This is bullshit! I'm going straight to the police, and we're going to put that asshole in prison," my dad was screaming.

"Jim, calm down!" my mom yelled at him, wiping away a few tears from her face.

Ted, often the mediator in family situations, added, "Now, guys. We have to keep a cool head about this so we can do everything correctly and rationally. Branden needs our love and attention right now."

I noticed my mom's quivering lips from the corner of my eye. "I'm so sorry, Branden. I don't know what to say. I'm so, so sorry." She burst into full-on crying.

Ted spoke up again. "Lynda, you need to be calm. Branden—how would you feel about going to the police station this afternoon?"

I could only nod in acknowledgment and wipe away the droplets that were falling off the tip of my nose.

"Well, I'm going with you guys," my dad declared. "The police need to hear from me what a sick ass this man is!"

My dad was a very patient man, albeit stubborn. But when he reached his boiling point, all he could see was fury.

"Jim!" my mom yelled at him.

Ted chimed in: "I think Branden and I should go and handle this. We've got this under control."

My mom leaned forward as if to say something, but then stopped herself. She knew this was the best course of action, even though it irritated her that my uncle was involved. Sibling rivalry doesn't ever end, I don't think.

My mom stood up from the couch. "I need to get Ashley to her soccer game. Jim, get in the shower, get ready. We're leaving in twenty minutes. And Ted," my mom continued, "please take care of my son." She could hardly spit out the last few words, as grief had overcome her.

Ted and I sat around for a few more minutes while he made small talk with my dad, who quickly lightened the mood by cracking a few out-of-place jokes. That's his modus operandi when there is *real* emotion in the room. It's learned behavior from his dad, and I'm guessing it's a way for him to disconnect from the constant hell of chronic pain that he's been in for the last twenty-five years. I continued to sit there, stunned and ashamed about the whole thing. We left for the police station, and Ted comforted me on the way there. He reminded me that this would be a difficult road ahead, but it was nothing that we couldn't all get through together.

The police were also hell-bent on the idea that none of this was to be taken lightly, and they assigned a detective to the case. A few days later, she interviewed me back at Denny's. Apparently, I preferred to spill my darkest and deepest secrets over a chocolate malt at a low-rate diner franchise. My dad accompanied me at that interview. I told the detective about what had happened and gave them the man's business card. But the man had already left town by that point. And with no way to prove what had happened, I wasn't optimistic about a resolution.

We had come up with a plan as a family to file charges, but the detective reminded us that it would have been his word against mine, since I had just turned eighteen. My, how things have changed. When it comes to sexual assault these days, people's word is more likely to be taken at face value. But this was not necessarily so in 1996. The fact that I was eighteen would mean that if I did press charges, I would have to go to court and testify as my only proof—that is, if they tracked him down. After much deliberation, I made a decision not to proceed with the charges. I just wanted out of Southern California, and I wanted to leave all of this as a distant memory.

I took my future education opportunities seriously and decided I didn't want to see my face in my hometown news-papers. It was more practical for me to remain anonymous and start fresh in the Bay Area. But nowadays, my biggest regret in choosing not to come forward is simple: people who prey on younger people are often repeat offenders. I can't help but wonder: Were there others after me? Could I have stopped it? The unknown answers to those questions will haunt me for the rest of my life.

I found out recently, as I was texting my mom for her input on this story, that she could still provide names, places, even intricate descriptions of what happened. She was sharp like a mother wolf and keen on every need of her children. That *is* my mom, in essence. As she told me these details, I wondered why it takes us so long as offspring to see the inher-ent goodness in our parental figures. Why do we choose to ignore the love and protection and focus on the way our par-ents wronged us instead? My mom and my dad taught us love by *showing* us what love is. They were living examples of it.

What happened to me after high school is just what happened. It doesn't define me, nor define who I am. Neither does my sexuality define me, nor my gender, nor my HIV status. These are all just circumstantial things that happen in our lives—nothing more. Resilience was in my blood, and I was tough as nails after my childhood. Now it was time to pack up the family van and move north to find my new identity in music in the City by the Bay.

CHAPTER
SEVEN

We packed what I had, which wasn't much. My parents were able to spare an extra twin mattress and frame for me to use in a new apartment. This meant that friends and family visiting from out of town would be confined to my parents' pullout couch in the living room, but they didn't think twice about it. I gathered everything I thought I needed: warm clothes, shoes, music books, the photo album from high school my mom had made for me. I had the bare essentials and just a tiny bit of money saved up: enough to pay my first and last month's rent plus a security deposit. My parents, albeit on a shoestring budget, tend to make a vacation out of everything, so with my sister and me in the van, the four of us made our way north on the 101 freeway in leisurely fashion. This journey was a few hours longer, but it was much more picturesque and gave us more sights to reminisce over.

We arrived in San Francisco and buzzed around the city searching for a hotel, passing by the Conservatory of Music, the neighborhood of Cole Valley, and the Castro district. It was the first time I had seen a concentrated area with a largely LGBTQ population. A giant rainbow flag flew high and proud from the corner of Market and Castro Streets—the site where Harvey Milk was shot and killed. We drove and drove, trying to find something we could afford. We eventually went back to the school and asked about inexpensive accommodations in the area. The admissions officer, who was still charmed by my uncle Ted's previous encounter with her, came through with a guest house in a basement.

We checked in and spent about four nights there, huddled together in two beds with space heaters on, wrapped in woolen blankets. The cold, damp air of Northern California was not something that any of us were accustomed to.

That Friday was student orientation and class registration. There was a meeting for all the new students in a venue called Hellman Hall, our biggest performance venue. I noticed so many other gay guys in that meeting. Some of them were so open in their presentation that it made me uncomfortable—after all, I was a mere refugee from behind the "Orange Curtain" of conservative Orange County. I registered for musicianship, harmony, Italian, vocal performance lab, music history, vocal diction, opera workshop, and individual vocal instruction with my teacher, Johan Kruger. I tested out of my piano exams, so I had room for some extra credits.

Instead of taking extra courses, I set aside the time to get a job. I needed to support myself financially and didn't have much of a choice. I was hired as a receptionist at school, answering phones and transferring calls. The window of my tiny little office was right at the front entrance of the school, so it was a great way to meet people. I had a wonderful group of friends in no time.

My parents were determined to do two things before they left: find me a place to live and find me a good church. We all agreed it would be important for me to live near school, in the area known as the Sunset District. Renting an apartment in San Francisco, even in 1996, was extremely difficult. Still, my dad had faith and said, "God will provide for us. I am certain." We prayed together every night as a family, and by the fifth day, he was right. We found an in-law apartment, as they refer to them in the city. This type of apartment is usually in the back of the garage at the ground level of a house or apartment building. It had a microwave, refrigerator, and a modest bathroom. The garage had a hot plate and utility sink available to use as a stove and a place to wash dishes. It was separated into two bedrooms by make-shift closet doors.

The landlady, Carole, who also sometimes referred to herself as Barb, listed the apartment on the conservatory bulletin board for $550 per month. This was entirely out of our budget, but the place was directly across the street from my school, so we were determined to find a way to make it work. My dad, Ashley, and I roamed the halls of the music institute asking every random person if they were in need of a housemate. We came upon two very different people: Amid Mirwani, a master's degree candidate and American violist from the East Coast, and Mahmoud Tehrani, an Iranian guitarist who had just arrived in the United States.

After visiting with the two of them, I went with my parents' advice and chose Mahmoud. He spoke English fairly well. Amid was obviously gay, and that made my parents a bit nervous.

"That Amid kid seems a little high-strung, if you ask

me," my dad had contributed. He wasn't far off. Amid did have an uneasy energy that filled the whole room. But I think this was my dad's way of advising me to avoid living with a gay guy. So we chose Mahmoud in the end. Bless his heart—he was the hairiest kid I had ever seen. His back was like a rug, he had one eyebrow, and every inch of his fingers and toes was covered in thick hair. He was soft-spoken and wore thin, wire-rimmed glasses. He was interested only in practicing and working hard at his education.

I was also determined to excel in my studies, but I'd just had the bandage of a conservative family ripped off me and had landed in a progressive environment. I wanted to explore and meet people and go to Haight-Ashbury and wander down the streets of the Castro, where I'd spotted all of those rainbow flags. They say that the best kinds of roommates are the ones you're not terribly friendly with, but cordial with. This description fit Mahmoud to a T at first. We were simply living together, and that's about it. Over time, we developed a lovely friendship, however, and he came home with me one summer to explore the beaches of Southern California. It was a pleasure to live with him: he wasn't a snorer, he was fairly clean, and he lulled me to sleep every night with his beautiful guitar playing. The only drawback was the amount of hair he shed. It some-how ended up everywhere—in my sheets and on my pillow (although he never went into my room, to my knowledge), all over the bathroom, shower, and bathtub. I opened the microwave to heat up a frozen dinner on a cold night and even found his hair in our rapid cooker.

Next on my parents' list (well, my mom's in particular) was to find me a good church. It was important to my folks that I continue going every Sunday, even though I was well over it by this time. On a Saturday, we paid Carole/Barb the rent and moved all of my things into my new place. We went out that night for a burrito at a local taqueria to celebrate our thrifty find and got an early night's sleep in order to get to church on time the next day.

It was a beautiful, sunny Sunday when we trekked down to the marina district. We arrived at church a few minutes late, not anticipating traffic on a Sunday morning. The only seats left in the church were in the front row. We awkwardly made our way to the front row, and the pastor greeted us in a warm tone and said, "Welcome, my brothers and sisters." The service was similar to what we might have experienced at home: contemporary worship with hand raising and clapping, an offering, and a long-winded sermon that quoted Scripture in modern terms.

On the way into the service, I spotted the most handsome guy I'd ever seen. He was wearing tattered jeans, black boots, a light leather jacket, and a knitted beanie that highlighted his striking facial features. Sitting on the ground in the back of the church with his feet on the floor, his knees upright and his elbows dangling over them, he listened intently to the words of the pastor. During the sermon, I craned my neck to make eye contact with him and refresh my memory of his beauty. When the service was over, we attended the coffee and tea social and mingled with other parishioners of the church. The mysterious handsome guy came up to me, introduced himself as Logan, and gave me his number under the guise of offering me a ride to church the following Sunday. My face flushed when I noticed my mom watching me chat with him. Logan took off shortly after that, saying, "Call me. I'll pick you up anytime you like."

My parents, meanwhile, were talking to the pastor and his wife. The pastor's wife had a masculine build and a cropped haircut and was dressed in a pantsuit. The pastor, wearing a pink turtleneck sweater, introduced himself to me and asked if I would like to go to dinner at their house sometime. I politely accepted.

"I hope Branden can call our church home," declared the pastor.

"Yeah, so do we," replied my father. "He's a good kid."

I nodded in agreement, without an ounce of sincerity. My parents said their goodbyes and we left. My mom and sister had to get back to school and work the following day, so they dropped me off at my place to say goodbye for the last time. We exchanged long, tearful hugs. An immense fear of separation overcame me as I watched our blue van head south on Nineteenth Avenue, back toward Southern California. My sister, visibly crying, was waving out of the back window of the van. My mom had been crying since the first time I said, "You guys should get on the road." I was doing just the same. As eager as I was to go and find myself, I was equally frightened to leave the nest. The neighborhood I lived in was statistically safe, but a far cry from the bubble of Irvine. San Francisco was gritty and smelled of urine and its walls were covered in graffiti. I was living in a legitimate city now, and it both excited me and scared the hell out of me.

After a few hours of driving, my parents called me. Their voices were breaking. "Branden, we miss you so much already. We had to pull off the road and get a hotel for the evening. I'm just a mess. I didn't expect this to be so hard." I suppose with every kid that leaves home, the reality that your days of parenting are numbered becomes more apparent. This was number three of four children for my mom to say goodbye to. I was also mourning the separation from my best friend: my sister, Ashley. It killed me to think I wouldn't have her around as a companion or for an occasional brotherly tease when I needed one.

But I was an adult now, all on my own, pursuing a dream that was still a far cry from a reality. I did the first thing I knew how to: I went across the street and found a Mexican restaurant to comfort myself the way I knew best. The bill amounted to $6.75 plus tip, which I thought was very expensive at the time. After inhaling the budget meal, it was time to go to sleep—in the morning my new life at school would begin.

The first week of school was an overwhelming blur. Between working as many hours as I could (sometimes starting as early as six a.m. and then working after classes until eleven p.m.) and trying to absorb knowledge about important musical figures like Hildegard of Bingen, I was exhausted. But it soon became a routine, and when everything finally settled in, I had never felt more at home personally or professionally. I was lucky enough to carry over my title from high school as one of the best singers at the conservatory. It was a lifeline of confidence I desperately needed.

Meanwhile, my identity was evolving in other ways, as well. On Friday night after my first week of school was over, I had picked up the piece of paper and called the church guy, Logan, to ask for a ride on Sunday. The phone rang a few times.

"Hello?" he said in a brash tone.

"Um, hello. This is Branden. From church?" I spoke very softly.

"Branden!" His tone changed immediately. "Hey. How are you? I've been wondering all week if you were going to call."

"Yeah, sorry," I replied. "First week of school and all of that. So, do you still want to go to church on Sunday?"

"Sure," Logan said. "I can still pick you up if you'd like."

"Would that be okay?" I asked coyly.

He giggled a bit over his reply. "Yes, of course that's okay." I'm sure he could sense my nerves on the phone. This was uncharted territory for me. We both knew that church was a euphemism for a date, but we went to church anyhow. He picked me up early on a Sunday morning, after I'd been out the night before at a house party with some new friends from school. An older undergraduate student had thrown a soirée in his apartment nearby, and I had gone just to get my feet wet. He had prepared a vodka lemonade cocktail that was spiked with black pepper. It was quite a bougie con-coction, and he certainly didn't know his alcohol-to-mixer proportions, because I was well overserved.

The both of us had ended up getting a bit frisky with a girl who was at the party. Much to our chagrin, we each received a phone call from the girl a few weeks later explaining that she had contracted an STI around the time that she had slept with us. We joined forces to find a clinic and seek immediate testing and treatment. We were delighted when we were eventually informed that our tests were negative, but the two of us left the clinic that day with a giant dose of humility. Even in 1996, STI testing was much more archaic than it is today. The tool required to conduct the test was a long wooden swab with a metal brush on the end of it that resembled a Brillo pad. This swab was meant to go down our meatuses. For those of you who don't know what a meatus is, look it up. Needless to say, the pain involved would teach any rational person to drink less vodka and more lemonade in future.

So that Sunday morning I wasn't in the best form to meet Logan for our church date. There was a special make-shift doorbell that Carole/Barb had made so people could ring for me when they were at the street entrance. It was a grating ring to begin with, which was only exacerbated by a hangover. Not to mention it startled my roommate Mahmoud, who was hearing the bell for the first time. He came running out in his flannel boxers without his glasses on. That was the first time I'd seen him fully disrobed. It was like the second coming of Chewbacca. I pulled myself together and even grabbed my leather-bound Bible that my mom had made for me before I went charging for the apart-ment gate.

Logan was standing there, dressed down, but stylish like a New York club kid. *Who is this guy?* I thought. When we arrived at church, Logan elected to sit in a chair this time instead of on the floor. I'd never been on a date at church. Well, I take that back. I have if you count the times I went to church with my high school girlfriends, but that was all pretense. I certainly had never been to church with another openly gay man. Worship commenced, and a few songs were played that I knew. Logan kept moving his head closer to my mouth to hear me sing. This left me bashful, and I made myself quiet down.

After church we went to lunch at a local comfort food joint in the Castro, which also happened to be his workplace. We sat there for hours just talking about life and his former career. To my utter surprise, he revealed that he was thirty-four years old. I'd thought he was in his early twenties! Logan told me all about his former career as a dancer at the Metropolitan Opera. He reminisced on the wildest stories about some of the greatest opera stars, and about the things he did onstage, right in front of the audience, that no one ever knew about.

His second job was as a driver for a nearby mortuary. It was like something straight out of *Six Feet Under*. He had to collect bodies from hospitals and morgues and bring them to the mortuary. He remarked at how well an eighty-year-old dead man's endowment was preserved, despite the wrinkles on the rest of his body. His stories, off-color and filled with macabre humor as they were, turned my stomach a bit. I wasn't interested in getting closer to death; it was still something I feared at my age. We wrapped up our conversation, and he asked if I wanted to check out his place, since it was just around the corner. We strolled into a Victorian-style apartment building not far from the mortuary where he worked.

Inside, he lit some Nag Champa incense and showed me around his place, including his prized photos from his dancing days and photos he'd taken with opera stars in scanty costumes. I stood there trying to imagine myself singing in a show at the Metropolitan Opera one day. Logan, who was nearly twice my age, embraced me from behind and kissed my neck, which I welcomed. This time, it wasn't uncomfortable or violating. It felt the way I always imagined it would: natural and sublime.

After things died down a bit, we lay in his bed and he shared with me his newfound Christianity. He had only been born again for three months. "I can't help it," he admitted. "I know I'm not supposed to be doing this. It's unnatural. It's not God's will, but sometimes it's hard to fight." They'd been teaching us at church about the danger of having impure thoughts, let alone acting on them.

It all suddenly came together. *Did my parents take me to a church of homosexual reform? They must suspect I'm questioning my sexuality and didn't want to leave me in a place like San Francisco without some proper support.* I'd noticed several gay people there both times I attended, and I wasn't buying the relationship between the pastor and his wife at all. He was entirely too interested in me when we spoke.

Then again, maybe my parents didn't know. They were married at a church owned by the same group, and perhaps my mom knew the brand and thought that was a safe place to leave me. To this day, I've never spoken to her about it. I've never asked her if she knew the style of doctrine they taught at that church or whether her motivations were calculated. I'm still afraid to ask, if I am honest. At this point, I don't want to know.

I saw Logan a couple more times after that, but I soon got a paid job at a Catholic church and stopped going for the other weekly services. Our age gap made it hard to connect on any substantive level, and there was a guy at school who I was interested in named Michael. He was a percussionist. I guess I have a thing for fellow musicians, seeing as how I eventually married a cellist. Michael and I dated at the same time I was dating two other girls at school. Talk about a scandal in a student body of a mere 250 students. Scandal was of no concern to me, though; I was still finding my way through everything.

The first semester ended rather triumphantly for me. I passed my freshman vocal juries, aced all of my courses except for harmony, and was cast as Don Basilio in the school spring opera, *The Marriage of Figaro*. I made some dear friends, including Hannah Rutledge, a red-headed soprano who had one of the most powerful voices I'd ever heard live. We shared personal details with one another and became instantaneous family. We'd often drive around the city with the windows down and belt out operatic arias on busy street corners before stepping on the gas, leaving everyone in wonderment on the streets as to where those voices were coming from. Michael and I had also forged a beautiful friendship with Ingrid Olsen, a stunning blonde Norwegian violinist who was insanely talented and such a joy to be around.

To celebrate my academic success, I went for a hike at Land's End with Michael, whom I was exclusively dating at this point. This is where you insert the falling-off-a-cliff story from earlier in the book. Yes—that was the day I skipped down a hill, fell off a cliff, and broke a bunch of bones, which led to a series of operations on my left ankle. I had to drop out of the school opera because the director couldn't justify the character of Don Basilio on a pair of crutches.

My mom took two weeks off work to come up for my surgery and to nurse me back to health. She has always been wary of anesthesia. There was even more reason to be wary in my case, considering my future aspirations as an opera singer. So instead, I had an epidural. I was bound to my bed following my release from the hospital, and just a couple of days into my recovery period, I discovered that I had remarkably painful migraines. They were especially bad when I would sit up. If I were lying flat, I could get some relief. But otherwise, my pain was excruciating. My mom called my young surgeon and explained what was happening, and he ordered further tests: an MRI, CT scan, blood tests, and the whole lot. It took ten days for them to figure out that there was actually a leak in the patch of my epidural. Spinal fluid was leaking from the puncture site, and that was causing the pain.

As most healthy teenagers would do, I recovered swiftly from this setback and was out of my cast just twelve weeks later. The pins and screws were removed about six months after that, and I would suffer no lasting side effects except for arthritis when I got older. My doctor promised that would happen. I'm still waiting for it to come. Every once in a while, I can sense a cold front coming in, or moisture collecting in the air. My ankle stiffens and loses some dexterity.

That summer, I was cast as Tamino in the opera theater production of *Die Zauberflöte*, or *The Magic Flute*. I was eager to get onstage and play my first major role. There were children of all ages involved in this summer workshop, as well as college students. My voice teacher managed to get my sister a scholarship to the program, and she was cast as the second spirit in the same production. So again, we shared the stage together, and my mom, sister, and I spent two long weeks together in my studio apartment.

When the opera performances finished, I went home for the rest of the summer, initially bringing my secret boyfriend Michael down with me, and then later Mahmoud.

While Michael was there, he would come crawl into bed with me in the middle of the night for a cuddle, and then go back into his guest room before day broke.

Michael was a bit of a tech nerd. At his apartment, he had a first-edition Mac computer with a small camera overhead. He introduced me to Gay.com and online chatting as a way to meet people. Michael's parents were wealthy people who hailed from New Mexico. His father held a prestigious position at a hospital. We went out to the desert a few times, and I experienced what real privilege felt like. At one point, he left school for a semester to spend time at home in New Mexico. While he was away, I made some friends outside school and discovered one of the popular gay bars in San Francisco's famous Castro district.

The Café was perched on the second floor above a series of restaurants and shops near the corner of Eighteenth Street and Market. Sunday afternoons were my favorite time there. They had a T-dance every week, which is essentially a daytime dance party. From the second-floor balcony, I would watch time lapse from day into night as the fog crept over Twin Peaks from the ocean and covered the Victorian houses dotting the craggy hills. You could barely make out the twinkling lights of the dwellings on the hill, but an oversized rainbow flag reigned supreme in the view, like a beacon on the busy street corner.

That bar became my happy place. We were all like family there: it was my chosen family. Very few of us were out to our parents, and many of us weren't comfortable coming out in our current environments. Even in an open and affirming city like San Francisco, in the late nineties, revealing your sexuality did not give you a safety net. But at the Café, we were safe and we were loved, and we gave love to one another. It was the most beautiful human experience I had ever seen: each of us as outcasts, supporting and caring for one another.

CHAPTER

EIGHT

A nother school year flew by. Rather than spend my second summer at home in Orange County, I decided to stay in the city and get an off-campus job to earn extra money. I didn't mind my high school position as cashier at Knowlwood, so I thought I'd stick with the restaurant business. I typed up a meager résumé and took it around to various restaurants on the busiest street in the Sunset district, Irving Street. I ended up landing a position at Pluto's restaurant. I mostly worked at the grill preparing fresh chicken, steak, salmon, and portobello mushrooms as toppings on people's salads and protein plates.

In the Outer Sunset, where I lived, the sun rarely came out, so I often froze on the bike ride to work and back. It may as well have been Glasgow, Scotland, and I found the weather to be terribly depressing. This may seem like an exaggeration, but to a Southern California beach boy, it was a menacing climate. The ocean wind and moisture just cut right through me. The job was grueling and sweaty, and I was tired of hearing patrons' complaints that I was taking too long to get the food on their plates. *How about next time you don't order well-done steak, jerk? How can you be allergic to oil, butter, garlic, onions, tomatoes, seeds, alcohol, and vinegar, lady?* These are the things I would say in my head while they were inevitably bitching at me for getting it all wrong.

There were some pleasant encounters as well, but it was mostly thankless work. Between standing over the flame of the hot grill all day, the awkward working hours, moaning customers, and the bone-chilling fog, I became quite depressed. I promised myself that I'd never do that again over the summer. Michael, along with most of my friends, went back to their hometowns that summer. Meanwhile, I was doing the same thing day in and day out, six days a week. I wasn't singing. I wasn't socializing. I was just existing. When late July rolled around, I dusted off some of my books of German *lieder*, French *chansons*, Italian art songs, and operatic arias. My third year in college would be my first big test in that I'd be putting on a required, public junior voice recital. The scheduled opera for the season was *Die Fledermaus*, and I desperately wanted to play the part of Alfredo, so I listened to the music over and over on CDs I'd acquired from the school library.

Despite my misery, it's as if I blinked and summer was gone. I happily quit at Pluto's. Michael came back a few weeks before the school year commenced, and we found an amazing apartment on Fifteenth and Kirkham and officially decided to live together. He wasn't right for me on so many levels, but he led a comfortable lifestyle with his parents' fortune, and I was the beneficiary that it often trickled down to.

The other reason I stayed was I think I'd finally overcome dating girls. Up until then, I had gone on dates with several girls at school: a Russian mezzo-soprano, a Bay Area coloratura soprano, and a Latina soprano from Ventura County. I had a thing for singers, too, I guess. My emotional connection with these girls was electric, but I would avoid a physical encounter whenever I could. When we had intimate moments, I was fantasizing about the oboe player Adam, or the trumpeter from Oklahoma named Christian. I figured that was a good sign—that I was coming to terms with my sexuality. I explained my living situation to my parents as just roommates, of course, but the domestic goddess in me had me decorating and painting, cooking, throwing dinner parties, and making use of the apartment as a proper home. It was well out of my budget, but I paid what I could, and Michael's parents picked up the slack.

In previous years, the conservatory loaned full-size pianos to students who wanted to use them at home to practice on. The only catch was that the student had to pay for the moving and shipping of the piano and then return it before they left school. When I left my previous apartment, my landlady told me, "A student from seven years ago left this piano here and I'd love to get rid of it. If you can move it, it's yours." The piano rightfully belonged to the conservatory, but they had forgotten about it. I cleared the idea of keeping it with my voice teacher, and he didn't see a problem with it, so I moved it into our new apartment, and it became the focal point of many singalongs at our parties.

We cherished that apartment and had a cast of regular visitors there. The most frequent visitor was Ingrid Olsen, the Norwegian violinist I met as a freshman. The three of us became inseparable. She was the yin to our yang, and despite her conservative religious views, she embraced us and even joined us in her birthday suit at Baker Beach, the nude beach just under the Golden Gate Bridge, where we'd cut class on warm days. Both Ingrid and Michael were two years my senior, which meant they turned twenty-one when I was still under the drinking age. Occasionally, they'd go to the neighborhood watering holes together, and when they did, I got a taste of what real jealousy felt like. Being under the drinking age in college absolutely sucks when all your friends are out at the bars.

It was an incredibly fruitful school year. I got the part I wanted in *Die Fledermaus*. I was the only undergraduate student to get a lead in the opera, and I sang it with all my might. It was my first foray into comedic acting, and much to my surprise, people found me funny. My junior recital was filled with the music of Schubert, Donaudy, Duparc, and some traditional spirituals. One graduate baritone said to me in his southern drawl, "I think that was just about the best recital I've ever seen here." I was beaming, and I couldn't believe how much I was thriving.

Year three was when opera performance students would delve into the German language after having spent the previous two years studying Italian and French. I enjoyed exploring new languages so much, except for French. Today, I love to sing in French, but I was never any good at understanding the grammar of the language. It just confused the hell out of me to stare at words with ten or eleven letters and be told to only pronounce half of them. But I was taken with German *lieder* and found them so immensely satisfying to sing. The color in the harmonies of the composers Schubert, Schumann, Strauss, and Wolf just made me swoon. I couldn't get enough of it, nor could I stop exploring the works of my two favorite romantic British composers, Roger Quilter and Ralph Vaughan Williams.

Offers for gigs were flying in for me: private concerts, appearances at wineries, solo jobs at churches for Handel and Bach oratorios. This, in addition to my regular church jobs, provided a decent income for a student like me. It was sometimes challenging to navigate the entire Bay Area without a car, but I didn't mind spending time on public transportation. I had saved up some money and bought myself a Discman to pass the time.

One day, while wandering the halls at school and peering through various practice rooms to see who was playing what, I came across a notice on the school jobs board that Max's Opera Cafe on Van Ness Avenue was hiring servers who could sing. I thought, *Hey, why not?* My friend Hannah was a waitress at the sister location in San Bruno and had always boasted about how much money she made. I didn't have any serving experience at that point, only menial restaurant work, but luckily I could sing my way through the audition and scored the job immediately. I was a scattered and terrible server, and the stoic general manager absolutely loathed me, but she *needed* me there for my voice.

And so I persisted for about a month or so, until I got an unexpected phone call at home. "Hi, Branden, it's Alycia from Max's."

"Oh, hi, Alycia!" I replied. She was another waitress there—an unusually tall, red-haired girl in her late twenties with a low contralto musical theater belt.

"Hey, I know this man named René who music directs

for a hotel in Switzerland, and he's looking for a tenor for a singing waiters gig there. Would you be interested? It starts in two weeks."

Switzerland? In two weeks? Wait a minute. How is that going to work? I still had a few weeks left of school to finish, my final exams most importantly. I'd never had a passport, nor had I been out of the country, except for the time I took a chartered bus to Mexico with my high school youth group to help build an orphanage outside Ensenada. I'd only been on a plane a couple of times, and suddenly I was being offered a job in Switzerland?

My curiosity got the best of me and I said, "Of course I'd be interested. How do I audition?" She explained that she was also going to do the gig, but that René, the music director, was currently living and working in Switzerland.

"I mailed him my materials. I'm sure you can do the same thing." Alycia was a lovely girl with a big heart, but she was a little ditzy at times. I was twenty years old. I didn't have *materials.* Nor was I going to be able to generate them in time to send them to Switzerland for someone to review within two weeks.

"Why don't you give me his contact information, and I'll figure out the best way forward," I suggested. I thanked her profusely for thinking of me and hung up the phone.

Suddenly, the enchantment of going to live and work in a foreign country occupied all of my thoughts. I called my friend Christina and buzzed with elation about the idea. I called my mom and told my friend Hannah as soon as I saw her at school.

"But the school year isn't over yet," she noted.

"I know. I know, but maybe there's a way around it. Can

you imagine? Living in Switzerland? How much fun would that be?" I said.

Hannah squinted at me skeptically. She couldn't imagine doing something like that. In fact, she had never left the state of California. I called Alycia and told her that I would like to have a conversation with René. She got back to me almost immediately, and I prepared for the call. I lay awake with excitement that night, unable to sleep because my thoughts were filled with grandiose images of what it was like to live in Europe. This gig would also be my first *real* professional gig, and the thought of that was equally thrilling.

That morning around nine a.m., I called René. I kept thinking of how astronomical the phone bill would be if it were a long conversation. The phone rang, but it wasn't the typical American phone ring—it was a long, sustained, slightly softer tone. Just hearing *that* difference made me tremble with delight.

"Hello?" a friendly voice answered on the other side.

"Uh. Hello. This is Branden James. I, uh, am supposed to call you…"

"Branden!" I was interrupted by a woman's voice, who was also on the phone. Judging by their accents, both René and this woman were American.

"Hi, I'm Maya. I'm the vocal captain of the singing waiters here in Interlaken." *Interlaken. Now I can research where this gig is*, I thought.

"Thanks for calling us all the way from San Francisco," René said. "So Alycia told you a little bit about what the gig is?"

I replied, "Not really. She just mentioned something

about a quartet of singing waiters. And just so you know up front, I'm not the most experienced waiter, if this is in some fancy restaurant or something. I just started serving for the first time a month ago."

Maya chuckled in the background and said, "Don't worry, you're not *actually* a server, you're just dressed up like one. This is a singing and performance job only. Well, for the most part. René, can you explain further?" René explained that I was to be part of a vocal quartet who sang everything from vocal jazz to show tunes to pop arrangements, and we were also required to sing solos and duets in the restaurant four nights a week, from six p.m. to nine p.m. "Alycia mentioned that you're a great baritone."

I rolled my eyes and took a long pause. "Branden?" Maya asked after me.

"Uh…" I've always said *Um* and *Uh* when I'm nervous. It has never changed, to this day. I must sound like a blithering idiot on the phone.

"Umm. I'm not a baritone, unfortunately. I'm a tenor. There must've been a mistake. Thanks anyway for taking the time."

Immediately saddened, I reached to hang up the phone.

"Wait!" Maya yelled. "Hey, Branden? It sounds to me like you have a very resonant speaking voice. What's your range?"

I answered automatically without thinking. As a pompous collegiate opera singer, I knew exactly what my range was. "I can sing a low F all the way up to a D above high C," I said.

"Wow! It sounds like you have an incredible range," René said, marveling. "Now, we lost our baritone to an opera contract at the end of our last session, and we could really use someone to fill the spot. Did Alycia explain to you that the gig starts in two weeks?"

"Yes," I replied.

"Are you in school?" he asked.

"Yes," I replied again.

"When is your last day of school?"

"May 15?" I said, unsure whether they would accept that.

"Oh. Well, we'll get to all of that in a minute. Now, I'm not sure if you're prepared for this part or not, and we normally don't do it this way, but Branden, would you mind auditioning over the phone for us?"

Over the freaking phone? They want me to sing into the phone to get a job? This is ridiculous! I thought.

"Of course I wouldn't mind!" were the actual words that came out of my mouth, although they weren't the truth.

Maya chimed in again. "Are you warmed up?"

"No, not really. I just woke up a little while ago." I started to get nervous.

"No worries. Can you hear this piano René is playing? *Play, René!*" I heard her command him in haste. A few impressive, jazzy chords chimed through the phone.

"Yes, I can hear it," I answered.

"Great!" exclaimed Maya. "I'm going to give you some exercises to sing that will warm you up. You just repeat after me."

Maya started singing in a beautiful soprano voice on the vowel aah. She gently took me down to the bottom of my register and then reversed and went all the way up. We vocalized exactly to the places I said I could—low F to D above high C.

"Dude. You have an amazing range. Holy shit," she said.

René spoke again as if to make up for her profanity. "Do you feel like you're warmed up enough to sing us something from your repertoire?"

"Um. Uh. Yeah, I think I could do that."

They couldn't see me, but I was tearing around the house with the phone wedged between my neck and my right shoulder, trying to find something to sing, anything. Sitting on the piano was my giant turquoise fakebook of all of the great songs from musical theater. A fakebook is a book filled with melody lines, lyrics, and chord symbols. That's it. This was an excellent tool for me, given that I hated playing the actual notes on the page, a trait that had carried over from childhood. I had been studying up on the music from Rodgers and Hammerstein's beloved musical *Carousel* because my voice teacher had mentioned that it might be the spring musical next year.

"How about 'You'll Never Walk Alone'? In C major?" I asked.

René answered enthusiastically, "That's a fantastic song! Go right ahead."

I put the cordless phone on the dining room table. I thought that if I placed it there, perhaps the piano and the vocals would be better balanced. Sitting down on the loose, squeaky piano bench, I played a two-bar intro, and then off I went, tentatively of course. That was me—tentative. Not to mention it was still awkward to think that two Americans in *Switzerland* were on the other end of the phone critiquing me.

I launched into a full croon. One of the secret weapons in my voice is that there's little distinction between my chest voice and my head voice. This means that when I cross my break, which is also known as a *passaggio*, or bridge, I can flip effortlessly into my head voice, but it still sounds like my full voice. This ability, by the way, is fading, and like everything in life at forty years old, I have to work harder for it. But at the time, I went for it: I sang alternate notes on the last phrase reaching all the way up to high C, and then finished on a long, sustained G. When I finished singing, I picked up the phone, and there was silence that lasted for a good twenty seconds. I started to worry that maybe I'd lost connection with them.

Then Maya, with a broken, emotional voice said, "Branden. You have such an incredible gift. You've moved me to tears. I'm lost for words."

René said, "Branden James. How old are you?"

"I'm twenty years old," I answered.

"Wow, sir. You have an incredibly mature voice for your age."

I was used to people telling me this. My voice teacher, Johan Kruger, and I had been working fastidiously to brighten my sound, because my tendency was to "sing like a baritone," as he named it. This was probably some internal attempt to sound more masculine. René went on, telling me how much the gig paid and when I was needed in Switzerland for rehearsals. I was gobsmacked when he told me how much. To think I only had to work fifteen hours a week to earn that kind of money? I thought for sure this was the big-time.

"Why don't you speak to the conservatory about all of this, and then we'll call you back in two days to check on everything. Sound good?"

"Yes. Yes! This sounds amazing. Thank you guys so much. I'll do the best I can."

I hung up the phone, dashed through a shower, and raced to school to blow the whistle. I knew exactly who to go to first: Janine Greenblatt. After all, she was the one who'd permitted me to audition without so much as a single application. I rushed into her office and explained what was happening.

"Leave it with me," she said. "I'll speak to the dean and I'll have an answer for you in an hour. But Branden, wait!" she exclaimed. "It will be up to you to convince your teachers. You still have to finish your courses and take all of your exams. I don't have control over any of that."

I nodded and went racing past the receptionist, Pearl Goodman, straight down the hall and into a practice room. I could hear the dulcet tension of Ingrid's violin in a room just down the hall. "Ingrid! Ingrid!" I probably made her think there was some sort of emergency.

"What? What is it?" she asked as she carefully set her violin on the piano.

"I was offered a job in Europe! Singing!"

"Where?" she gasped.

"In Switzerland," I yelled, my voice reverberating off the practice room walls.

"Woo-hoo hoo hoo hoo!" She belly laughed and blushed as only a Norwegian could do and gave me a giant hug of congratulations. I let Ingrid get back to her practicing and sat on the bench in the front lobby, waiting for word from the dean. My right leg was shaking with nerves and excitement, and I kept my eye on the clock as other students rushed through the corridor. As soon as the clock struck one, I jumped off the bench, even though I was in midconversation, and ran back into Janine

Greenblatt's office. I walked in, and she had a big smile on her face.

"The dean said it's fine with her. As long as you pass all of your exams and work it out with your teachers, you're free to go!" I couldn't believe it. I got a job in Switzerland! Now, all I had to do was convince my teachers that going to be a singing waiter was more important than finishing the last couple of weeks of my junior year.

When I was in high school, I secretly thought of myself as a master manipulator. It was harsh, to be honest. I think I was simply a kind person, and people could see that. So when I asked for things, I generally was granted them. I was fortunate enough to have the same luck with all of my teachers at school. Some were more reluctant than others, but in the end, all of them approved of me skipping out to go fulfill my European fantasy.

I still had one difficult task left: I needed to convince Michael that it was the right move for me to make. He was off campus that day doing a string quartet gig for a funeral in the East Bay. He came home after dinner, and I was sitting at the dining room table when he walked in the door. I explained everything to him—the opportunity, the gig, the travel, the money. He wasn't having any of it.

"Well, if you want to live here, you're still going to have to pay rent over the summer," he scoffed. "I don't understand why you would leave school early to go off to Europe for four months. To do what? Be a singing waiter? You have so much going for you here." His tone was desperate, as if I was leaving him forever.

"Michael, come on. Please. You have to understand. This is my first *big* gig."

He rolled his eyes and chortled condescendingly. "I've been to Europe tons of times with my parents. France, Germany, Italy, the UK; I don't think you'll like it."

But his patronizing tone backfired and made it easier to make my decision. "This is the right thing for me to do. I can feel it. I'm going. End of conversation." That night I slept in the spare room on the twin bed, and he was out on the futon where we usually shared a bed. I felt so guilty, and I kept wondering, why? What had I done wrong? I suppose I understood why he was upset with me, but there was nothing anyone could say that would hold me back from exploring the world—nothing.

I lay awake that night shifting between excitement and guilt and wondering which Michael I'd wake up to the next morning. In a shift of character, he cracked open the door to see if I was awake. When he saw me sitting up in bed, he said, "I'm sorry, sweetie. I shouldn't have acted that way. Of course you should go to Europe."

I gave him a long hug and jumped in the shower. I had to visit the US passport agency in downtown San Francisco that morning to see if I could apply for a rushed passport. I took the train down to the Civic Center stop and waited in line for three hours before I got to the window. I presented all the necessary materials: birth certificate, Social Security card, proof of residence, and the two passport photos I had taken at Walgreens just before I walked into the office. It was $199 to rush my passport to me within ten days. This would only leave a three-day margin for error. I had several more conversations with Maya and René, signed and faxed a contract to them, and was all prepared to go.

The next ten days were grueling. I had to get the curriculum ahead of time from my teachers, write papers and essays, and take my final tests early. I was so determined to make all of this work that I ended that year with the highest GPA of my life: 3.99. Next stop: my new life in Europe.

CHAPTER
NINE

'''ve been to Europe countless times since that first job at twenty years old. I've lived and worked in the UK, Portugal, Belgium, and Switzerland, of course. I had a three-and-a-half-year relationship with a British guy named Ross and made my home in Worthing in West Sussex for a time. I'm currently on a plane headed for the Canary Islands, the collection of small islands just off the coast of northern Africa that belong to Spain. I'm no stranger to Europe—it's been a part of me for half of my life now. I'm at home when I'm there.

But when I first flew Air Canada from San Francisco to Zurich via Toronto, I was overwhelmed with a new sense of freedom. Simply being on the first leg of the flight to Canada and hearing the safety announcements in both French and English gave me the realization that there was a whole world out there I had never seen. I was the first in my immediate family to travel abroad—and the first to receive a college degree, come to think of it.

On my connecting flight to Switzerland in Toronto, I finally met Maya, the girl on the phone. Shortly after she auditioned me from half a world away, she went to her family home in Michigan for a holiday before starting her next contract. When she came to the front of the plane and introduced herself, I wouldn't have thought that we would go on to forge a deep friendship that has lasted all of these years.

Maya sat next to me and said in her no-nonsense, Midwestern accent, "Hey. You must be Branden."

"Um. Hello. Yes. Yes, I am."

"Hi!" she exclaimed. She had a bright face framed by dark, curly hair, perfectly white teeth, and glassy blue eyes. She had such a warm and welcoming voice, you couldn't help but be drawn in. "We're so happy to have you with us. I hope you love Switzerland, and Interlaken in particular. It's a very special place."

I stared at her, doe-eyed. "I hope so, too. I have no idea what to expect, but I'm definitely looking forward to it," I said with a dreamy expression and a half smile. I could only picture scenes from *The Sound of Music.*

"Anyhow," Maya continued, interrupting my daydream, "we have a lot of work to do, but don't worry. We'll make sure you're well prepared and taken care of."

I just stared into her eyes, mesmerized by her energy and her beauty.

"How old are you, by the way?" she asked.

"I'm twenty years old. I'll be twenty-one in June!" She started laughing.

"Well, that will be an anticlimactic birthday!" she guffawed. I raised my brow curiously. "The drinking age is eighteen in Switzerland. So that means I can buy you a beer as soon as we land."

I must admit, the excitement of it all was overwhelming. I actually enjoyed the long-haul flight. Today, you couldn't pay me to get excited about a flight that's over five hours. The only saving grace is the free glass of wine that's served with the mediocre food. It's the little things. When we landed in Zurich, Maya played den mother to me and Alycia, who was also on the plane. She helped us gather our things and used her own petty cash to buy our train tickets.

"We're going to take a train to Interlaken. The journey is about three and a half hours, and we'll have to change trains just once in Bern. You're welcome to sleep, of course, but it really is a beautiful ride." I could tell how proud she was to have lived in Switzerland for the past two years. On the long ride to the Alps, she pointed out various landmarks, the names of certain towering mountains and vast lakes, and a few waterfalls that you could see in the distance. She also gave us the lay of the land as far as our rehearsal process was concerned and spoke honestly about our modest accommodations and food options.

The Victoria-Jungfrau Hotel in Interlaken was home to a hotel school, which educated more than five hundred hospitality candidates from Ireland, Portugal, Germany, Macedonia, the Ukraine, and others. We were allotted three meals a day in the hotel canteen, where we had to eat among all of the other employees. Our accommodations were private, dorm-like apartments with stunning views. As the youngest member of the cast, and a boy at that, I was given a small apartment-hotel room with twin beds on the third floor. The ladies were all given top-floor apartments with both a queen bed and a twin bed for guests. They had walk-in closets and balconies with soaring views of the Eiger, the Monch, and the Jungfrau—the three iconic peaks that were visible for miles in any direction. Maya bragged from the beginning that she had a perfect view of the Eiger from her toilet seat.

I quickly adjusted to my new life in Switzerland, finding a place where I could practice piano and a lone computer at a nearby towering eyesore of a hotel that provided a free yet slow internet connection. I was able to keep in touch with my mom and Michael using this computer, and I sent an occasional email to my uncle Ted. From time to time, Michael and I would also send each other old-fashioned handwritten letters. Although I was happy to be in a new place, I was still lonely and often wondered what he was doing in San Francisco. A few days into my contract, Maya and I were working out in the posh hotel gym when she asked me point-blank, "Do you like boys or girls?"

I decided to be brave and tell her the truth.

"To be honest, I'm more into boys these days." The words came out of my mouth quietly, and my head hung with embarrassment. I felt like I had done something wrong by telling her the truth.

She smiled. "I'm only asking so I know who to introduce you to." I was relieved there wasn't any judgment attached to her question. We finished our workout with her skater-butt exercises, which she had learned from the previous resident tenor, who was also a gay man. Lying on a mat, she got down on her back and raised her pelvis in the air and squeezed her cheeks together for about fifteen minutes. She encouraged me to get down and join her, which I did unsuccessfully. After about five repetitions, I lost my balance and fell over on my side nearly on top of her, which made us both erupt in laughter.

From then on, we became an unlikely but inseparable pair of friends. She'd fondly refer to me as Hoser, and I would call her my little Maya. When I would knock on her apartment door, she'd shout, "Come in if you're ugly!" from the other side. If ever we had a disagreement, she'd jokingly tell me to suck her left tit. Sometimes after work, we'd hit up the local disco, Schwarz & Weiss, and dance our cares away until it closed. Pining for a late-night snack, Maya would lead the pack of us to the town bakery, then badger the early-rising employees to not only let her into the bakery around four a.m., but to give her freshly baked *gipfel* croissants with chocolate inside to boot. In very bad and broken German, she would harass the workers for taking a break (*eine pause*) even while being in there with a gang of privileged (mostly) Americans. But because she was a singing waiter and her picture was plastered on billboards all over town, her celebrity status and the force of her personality held them in check. After several late-night visits, their boss eventually got tired of our charades and forbade the bakery workers from opening the door for her.

Maya and I went on hikes up the mountains, took long bike rides, and swam in the lakes of Thun and Brienz that literally interlocked the small town. We'd share stories over a beer and sometimes a spliff (marijuana cigarette), which she would get from people who were training at the hotel school. We'd go out to Balmer's Youth Hostel to spy on the man she formerly fell in love with, and she'd often party harder than I could. She called herself Tequila Mama until she got sick and found herself facedown in a gutter on a summer evening.

We'd lie on her bed while she clutched her black Raggedy Ann doll and tearfully regaled me with stories of her former singing partner, whom she lost to AIDS in the early nineties in San Francisco. She'd often repeat herself, but I didn't care. She was like a super-cool aunt, even a mom at times, who always made time for me, and I made time for her. Most of all, we bonded musically and forged a duet partnership that was a match made in heaven. She told me how much I reminded her of her former partner and even introduced me to a few of the songs he sang, which are still in my repertoire. She could be a tad overbearing to my twenty-one-year-old ears, but I didn't mind. She was unabashedly Maya: an überintelligent kindred spirit who loved music and people more than anything in life. Her heart was pure gold.

Maya could relate to me because we both felt as if we were cut off from a part of our own identity. Neither of us had access to who we really were. The two of us were "recovering" from our religious upbringings and could relate deeply to each other's scars, despite our age difference. Maya was having her own queer awakening, having just started dating a woman in Colorado. In a short time, my bond with her became much stronger than anything I could form with my own family.

In my Euro job, we had the weekends free and weren't required to return to work until Monday evening at six p.m. So I would often travel. I'd take trips to local cities in Switzerland such as Zurich, Bern, and Basel, I'd take a funicular up the Alps and spend time in the villages of Gimmelwald and Grindelwald. Often, I'd stay overnight in a tiny hostel, which had a window that opened up at night to a moonlit valley with nothing but stars in the sky and the soothing rush of waterfalls in the background. Sticking my head out that window, I would marvel at the sights I was seeing and the life I was living, as the smell of pastures and night air filled my senses. The hostel had one meal on offer for breakfast and dinner. If you didn't like what they served, you didn't eat. This of course was before the time when restricted diets were trendy. So those of us today who are gluten-free, dairy-free, meat-free, pescatarian, ovo-lacto vegetarian, etc., would have had to find a way to cope. For lunch, you were on your own.

Up and down the sides of the mountains, there were well-marked paths that included estimated hike times and levels of difficulty, and they were available for anyone who was up to it. There were natural drinking fountains everywhere: water that had escaped directly from melting glaciers. Many of the trails led to small Swiss houses and chalets that all sported perfectly groomed flower boxes and an array of tiny gnomes in their manicured gardens. These footpaths would wind through forests and waterfalls, rivers and sharp mountainsides. Many of them would lead to a farmer who was selling the cheese he made from his barn, or a lace-making craftswoman who also had a penchant for making delicious yogurt with fresh fruit preserves. If I searched hard enough with my nose, I could smell a baker every now and again and would knock on his door. Between the regular food sources and an hour or so of wandering, I could squeak out a delicious lunch.

I'd also go abroad and visit neighboring Italy, Germany, and France. It was only three hours on the high-speed train to Milan, and if I sat on the left side of the train, I'd get treated to a stunning view of the famous Lake Como, where George Clooney resides, and glide past the village where Giacomo Puccini was born. I visited the cities of Stuttgart and Düsseldorf, Paris, Strasbourg, Lyon, Florence, Venice, and Bologna. My language studies and natural skills served me well in all of these places. At the time, I was like a sponge who could pick up new lingo within seconds, and I had no fear in speaking it to natives.

A couple of months passed, and it was nearly time for my mom to come for a visit. She had no money to make it happen, but my great-uncle Jack on my dad's side provided her with a Delta Airlines buddy pass, which made her trip free, essentially. I wanted to find a thoughtful way to belatedly celebrate my birthday and make the trip special for her. I saved up my money to ensure the both of us could have a quintessential Euro vacation experience.

Her trip coincided with a Gershwin dinner concert we were performing and an outside gig at a sister hotel in Lucerne. Already, this promised to be a unique experience for her first trip to Europe. My mom arrived with tons of energy as she always does, and unpacked all of her things in my small dorm. It was the only cost-free place she could stay. She arrived the night of the Gershwin concert and sat there beaming as we sang "Summertime" and "Anything Goes" and "Someone to Watch Over Me" in the intervals of a twelve-course meal. I was amazed when she woke up the next day and didn't have any jet lag to speak of. I headed off for rehearsal that day and turned my mom loose on the village of Interlaken, supplying her with a little bit of spending money.

At some point in the first couple of days, her energy changed. It wasn't delayed jet lag, which can sometimes happen. She became isolated and quiet and distant. She wrote in her devotional journal and read her Bible. I started to find her stories about our family members and lessons from church to be completely irritating at times, even. This wasn't uncommon for her to do at home; my mom has always had a tendency to be chatty. I just assumed that it was natural at my age to be annoyed by my mom a little bit. Not to mention, when anyone's parent comes to invade a twenty-one-year-old's space for ten nights, things can get a little tense.

When we were in Lucerne, she teamed up with a friend of Maya's from Seattle who was also visiting at the time. My mom and Laurie couldn't have been any different from one another. Laurie was a bleeding-heart liberal from Seattle who enjoyed a carefree life in every sense of the word. She had no inhibitions, nor did she hold her tongue to spare anyone. My mom remarked to Laurie on one of their afternoon walks, "It seems like there are a lot of gay people here, huh?" Laurie found it a peculiar quip and told me immediately.

On my free weekend, I took my mom to Santa Margherita and Portofino in Italy. It was about a four-hour journey in total, and we stayed in a reasonable but charming pension that came on the recommendation of one of the other singers in my group. We enjoyed lying in the sun on the beach, walking through the art-filled coastal towns, and eating gelato three times a day.

We had the unfortunate incident of needing to run away from a man who I was eyeing on the ferry over to Portofino.

He was jaw-droppingly handsome and obviously keen for something. I have a tendency to stare at everyone; it's my way of studying a person. I just get so damned curious about everything. So I'm sure I was sending mixed signals on the boat. When we realized the man had been following us for some time after we got off the ferry, I used my best Italian and swore at him so he would leave. My mom just thought he was a crazy person. She still does, as far as I know. In her reminiscent way, she brings the story up every now and again. I think we're at a place in our relationship now where I can finally tell her the truth.

Unfortunately, despite our adventures and laughter and meals together, the awkward distance between us that weekend was obvious to both of us. Her trip came to an end when we returned to Switzerland. On her last night, she came into the restaurant and ate dinner at the place where I performed so she could see me sing one last time. The next morning, I escorted her to the train station for her seven thirty a.m. departure. We hugged goodbye, and she teared up a bit. This wasn't uncommon for her, especially when she knew it would be a while before she'd see me again. We spent a moment saying our goodbyes—her crying triggered me to do the same. I helped her with her suitcase and waved goodbye as the train pulled away from the station.

My first thought was to go back to bed. We'd been up fairly late the night before, and I was exhausted. When I returned to my apartment, I walked over to flip on the television to help me fall asleep. On top of the TV, there was a long, handwritten letter from my mom. I recognized her handwriting immediately. I opened the letter and started to read it.

Dear Branden, thank you for hosting me here in this beautiful country. You were so gracious and generous. I can't believe all of God's beauty that I have seen in the past ten days. I need to tell you something very important. I know that you are gay and that Michael is your partner. This is unacceptable in the eyes of the Lord, and our family will not tolerate it, either.

As I read, sharp pains darted through my head, and I grew a bit dizzy. This was always the sensation I felt when I got in trouble at school or knew I had done something that was very, very wrong. *How did she know?* That was the first question I asked myself. *Was it so obvious that Michael was my partner when I brought him home those two occasions? Was I not careful like I thought I was?*

I continued to read the letter, and it was filled with references to biblical parables of those who had suffered from their own mistakes: Sodom and Gomorrah, Mary Magdalene, et al. I was so upset, I grabbed the letter and went upstairs to Maya's room. I knocked quietly, knowing the others on the hall liked to sleep in when they could. She answered the door in her nightgown with one eye open. "Come in," she said in a raspy, tired voice, this time with no smile. Poor thing, I had just remembered that Sherry kept her up partying all night, so she'd only had a nap by the time I arrived.

I showed Maya the letter and she lay on her back on the bed, holding it above her head, reading the entire thing. Along the way, she reacted to certain sentences. "Oh" was her response at times. A long "Ooh" popped up sporadically, and an occasional empathetic "Aww" came out. She put the letter down, sipped on her glass of water, and said, "Your mom just outed you without your permission. I'm so sorry, hon. This must be a shock," she empathized in her northern Michigan accent.

I wasn't aware of the unwritten rules around the subject of coming out. Maya educated me a bit and told me that coming out was a very personal process, and it was up to the person at hand to decide when and if it was appropriate to tell their friends and loved ones. It was a code that most liberal society lived by, because they had empathy for those who were on their journey of discovering their sexuality. My mom wouldn't know what that language meant if it hit her in the face. She lived only by the word of God.

Maya and I spoke a little more about the issue and then decided that we both needed sleep. I went downstairs to my room, crawled into bed, and fell into a stupor that lasted six hours. I was emotionally spent. When I woke up, I reread the letter in its entirety. A deep anger ignited inside me. I kept the revelation to myself at work that night. In fact, Maya was the only one who knew about it for the entire time I was in Switzerland.

I let a few days pass before I addressed the issue. I went to the Metropole hotel next door and waited for a while, as my internet gateway to the outside world was occupied by someone else. When my turn came, I sat down, took a deep breath, and logged in to my Hotmail account. There was an email from my mom waiting in my in-box. She said she arrived home safely and was suffering from terrible jet lag. She thanked me again for a wonderful trip but didn't make any mention of the letter she wrote.

How dare she be so passive-aggressive about this? She took away one of the most important parts of my journey! I can't believe she would do this to me. I was fuming and took out all my aggression on the keyboard. I held nothing back. I told her how fucking terrible she was and that she should fuck herself. I went completely off the rails.

From that day forward, I decided not to have any more communication with my parents until I felt differently about the situation. Although it seemed petty at the time, it was probably a mature decision, because I needed the space, and confronting them would have only made things worse. I had never tasted pain and anger so devastating. I went back to the hotel to check my email a little while later. I read a couple of emails from my dad telling me how disappointed he was with the language I used and how much I had upset my mom.

Still enraged, I wrote back to him, "Michael and I may decide to have a baby one day. You guys are going to have to get a lot more comfortable with this situation. This is your problem to fix, not mine." I didn't show any remorse and remained defiant. I saw a couple of emails from my mom but refused to open them.

I partied for the next seven weeks of my contract, drowning myself in beer after beer, eating more of my feelings, and smoking as much weed as I could. On top of it being an unhealthy way to deal with emotion, it was also detrimental to my vocal health. But at the nimble age of twenty-one, my voice seemed to handle it just fine. My contract ended in early August, and I flew back to San Francisco, excited to start my last year of college. Over the summer, I received a surprise phone call from the opera director at the San Francisco Conservatory. She apologized for bothering me on my time abroad and explained why she was calling. They were hoping to put on a production of Rossini's *Count Ory* in the spring. I knew nothing about the opera. Count Ory was the title role in an opera that was vocally acrobatic in nature, and there were only a couple of tenors who could pull it off.

"Would you be interested in doing it?" she asked.

"Of course!" I said, elated.

"Great! We'd still have to audition you out of formality. But the part is yours if you want it. Branden, I have one more thing. Can we please keep this between us? I don't normally precast any of my operas, especially at the collegiate level, but this is a special circumstance."

"Yes, I promise not to tell anybody. Thank you so much for thinking of me!"

Michael picked me up from the airport when I landed in San Francisco after four months abroad. I was happy to see him but also a bit apprehensive. Unbeknownst to Michael, I had been on a few dates with a Swiss German boy over the summer. Maya and I called him *blumen boy* (flower boy) because he ran a flower shop in town with his ex-partner. After a few pleasant dates with the florist, I realized what else was out there and wasn't sure if Michael was the person I wanted to stay with. He often reproached me for wanting to be a carefree person, and it seemed like I was walking right back into a trap.

Michael had planned a special outing for us that would keep me awake until nighttime so I could get back on a normal sleep schedule. The first stop was our favorite Mexican restaurant, and then it was off to downtown to see the new *South Park* movie that had recently come out. Talk about a culture shock. I had just spent four months living a Swiss lifestyle, and the first thing I come back to is *South Park*? There were moments in the theater that day when I thought

I might have a breakdown from being so overwhelmed. I was accustomed to the European way, and it was going to take time to get used to the loud, brash American way again.

But I was also emotionally exhausted. I had no idea what the future held for my parents and our relationship. I was going to focus on my chosen family now and do my best to leave my parents behind. At school, I fully embraced my sexuality, and Michael and I publicly dated. I was comfortable and happy and loved there for being me. Frankly, at that time, I felt like I didn't need my parents at all.

CHAPTER
TEN

The school year started out beautifully. I was recharged from a summer in Europe and the envy of many at school. I got a job at a new gay restaurant in the Castro that had just opened, called JohnFrank. With my limited restaurant experience, the general manager decided to take a chance on me because, as he said, I was cute. I was relieved to win a job at this caliber of restaurant on my looks, since let's face it, it wasn't going to happen otherwise. The manager was so patient with me and taught me all of the fine points of proper French-style service. It was nothing like the factory that was Max's Opera Cafe, churning out matzo ball soup and corned beef sandwiches at record pace. John-Frank restaurant was such a refreshing environment to be in—open, affirming, accepting. We were all the same, and we all loved each other.

There were a handful of women who worked there, too, many of whom were older and treated me like I was their son. Women just seemed compelled to do this—and still do, to be honest. The hot new restaurant in town that received rave reviews from *The San Francisco Chronicle*, it opened at the peak of the dot-com boom. The restaurant was flooded with young, moneyed, straight foodies who had come from south of the Market and Marina districts to enjoy the festive New American cuisine.

Eventually, I gave in to my mom's phone calls and emails and made a weekend trip to visit my family for Thanksgiving. Nearly six months had passed since her visit, and we hadn't had any communication. But I didn't make the holiday comfortable. I was, let's face it, a rather snooty student who thought I knew everything, and at the time, I condescended to the rest of my family because I was in college. I was the first in my immediate family on track to complete my higher education, and I wouldn't let them forget it. Also being the first to travel to Europe, I threw my worldly experience in their faces whenever I could.

"Well, in Europe, they don't have preservatives in their food," I would say. "You don't have to pay for health care, and their wages are much higher." I'm sure much of my condescending attitude stemmed from unresolved anger toward my parents—my mom in particular.

After a long weekend filled with friends and family, it was time for me to go home. My parents and I hadn't discussed anything that had happened in recent months, and everything *seemed* just as it always was. With all of my relatives around, there wasn't time to delve into anything deep. My dad offered to take me to the airport that last day. We spoke few words to each other on the way. This wasn't unusual—my father has always been a man of few words. But after sitting in traffic for a while on the 105 freeway, he decided to lay into me.

"We haven't had a chance to discuss your lifestyle this weekend," he said.

The hair stood up on my arms. "My lifestyle?"

"Yeah, your homosexual lifestyle in the *gay bay*. You are sinning, Branden. When is it going to stop?" This was the first time anyone had confronted me in this way. *Lifestyle? When is it going to stop?* I had to repeat these questions in my head just to make sure I was hearing them correctly.

"I don't know what you mean. You think I *chose* this? Do you have any idea how difficult this is for me? Being gay? Disappointing my family and my church and, in your opinion, my God? Why would I choose that?"

He took a minute to process what I was saying, and I could see his face and neck slowly change in color, as if he were having an allergic reaction to something. He roared, with a rage in his voice I never knew he was capable of, "I'm so goddamned sick and tired of your attitude, you little shit. You think you're so high and mighty, living a life of sin up there with all of those homosexuals in the *gay bay*? Do you have any idea how much you've hurt your mom?" Every time he uttered those words, the "gay bay," it just made my skin crawl.

"Dad, I—"

He interrupted me. "You know what, I'm sick and tired of all of this." He was furiously changing lanes to get off the freeway. "I'm done talking to you about this. Fix it or don't bother coming home again." He stepped on the gas, cutting off the people in the right lane, and raced up the side of the road to the off-ramp of the freeway, ignoring the people who were honking at him and raising their hands in disbelief. He continued racing up the makeshift lane and made a sharp right turn at the corner, screeching into fast-moving traffic. Immediately on our right was a Mobil gas station. He sped into the parking lot and slammed on the brakes near the service area, where one can refill air in their tires and check their water levels.

"Get out of the friggin' car, you son of a bitch. You can find your own damned way to the airport."

He pushed me out of the car, and I hit the ground with a thud, landing on my tailbone. My backpack and carry-on luggage followed, as I lay on the ground in disbelief. Slamming my door shut, he put the car in reverse and raced out of the parking lot. *My father just threw me out of the car.* He used language that I never thought I'd hear directed at his own son.

I sat there for a moment in a state of shock. Some passersby noticed what had happened but kept walking and minding their own business. I peered across the street and saw a store called Compton Hardware. It was then that I realized where I was, and I scanned my surroundings for a place to go: McDonald's, a coffee shop, anything. I was in the neighborhood of Compton, Los Angeles—the neighborhood that was, in the nineties, on my parents' list of places to never set foot in, due to the violent crime rates.

I stood up off the ground, still shaking, and got my bearings. I felt helpless and naked. I noticed a set of pay phones to my right and reached my shaking hand into my pocket to pull out a few coins. I didn't know who I could call. I had a long list of phone numbers memorized, but most of them were family members. Finally it came to me: my friend Christina, whom I'd met at church. She wasn't too far away at Cal State Long Beach; maybe she was free to pick me up?

I checked my watch and thought, *Shit. I'm going to miss my flight one way or another at this point.*

Christina had recently visited me in San Francisco, and we'd had a spat of sorts. She had been getting on my nerves, and I'd said some pretty terrible things to her. What can I say? We were young and immature. Despite our last encounter, I knew she was the type of friend I could count on. To this day, if I ever needed anything, she'd be there. On a plane the very next day, even. She doesn't always have the means to do it, but she's the type of friend who would find a way. She has always had my back.

The phone rang, and the reality of what had happened sank in. I couldn't hold back the tears. "Hello?" her arresting voice answered on the other side of the line.

"Christina, it's Branden." She immediately heard the tears in my voice.

"What's wrong, baby? What happened?" I just started sobbing and sobbing. She let me cry for a little while without panicking. It hadn't been so long ago that I was visiting her at her beachside apartment in Long Beach, and I confided in her about my sexuality over a rolled joint and some red wine. She was quick to comfort me and sympathize. I eventually calmed down enough to catch my breath. "What's wrong, hon? Why are you upset?"

"My dad," I managed to get out. "He was driving me to the airport. He threw me out of the car, Christina." I paused and swallowed, taking in the reality of what had just happened. "He threw me out of the car…" I burst into tears again.

"Oh my God, baby. Where are you?"

I tried to get a view of the cross streets. "I'm in Compton

off the side of the 105 freeway. I didn't know who else to call."

"Well, I'll come and get you. Tell me how to get there. I have class at ten a.m., but I can be late. I'll make something up," she said.

"Are you sure? I don't want you to miss school."

"Branden. Don't be silly. Where are you going?"

"I need a ride to LAX."

"Okay, just find somewhere to go sit and give me about forty-five minutes. I'll leave right now."

"Okay, thank you so much."

I hung up the phone and tried to contain my crying. I didn't want to make it obvious that I was in distress. Looking for a place of refuge, I saw a yellow sign for Denny's just down about a block and a half. Yet again, the generic diner was my saving grace. I started walking to the restaurant and was offered blow and weed by a couple of guys on the street. I politely declined and kept walking with my head down. Cars were driving by at various speeds. Many drivers slowed down to stare at me, and others shouted things out at me.

When I reached Denny's, I realized that I needed to call the airline and tell them I wasn't going to make it in time for my flight. I went straight to the bathroom, splashed some water on my face, and found a pay phone with a phone book attached to it. In the front was a list of 800 numbers, and I located United Airlines. Luckily the phone call was toll-free, because I was nearly out of coins. After waiting on hold for about fifteen minutes, I told the airline that my dad's car had broken down and I wasn't going to make my midmorning flight. Luckily, there was an eight thirty p.m. flight. The female agent I spoke to said the flight wasn't full and I could most likely get on standby. Second crisis averted.

The next phone call I made was to my mom. I needed to tell her what had happened. She listened with sympathetic ears as I explained.

"I'm sorry that happened. But I can't blame your father for feeling this way. He's entitled to his views, and you have made things really difficult for us."

I pleaded with her again, "But Mom . . ."

I stopped just short of telling her I was sorry when she said, "How about Shane and I get in the car and drive up and spend the day with you until your flight? We can meet you at LAX." I was reluctant to see her and to face the situation we'd been avoiding all weekend. At the same time, I just wanted someone to hold me, and so the idea seemed attractive.

I agreed. "I'll be in the United terminal after Christina drops me off, I guess. Just have Shane come in and look for me. I'll try and sit somewhere near the departure doors." This was back in the day when it was still legal for someone to pull their car up to a departure area, put the flashers on, and sit for a while.

I sat at Denny's for a bit, ordered my usual comforting chocolate malt, sucked it down, and walked with a hurried pace back to the gas station so I wouldn't miss Christina. She arrived a little late in her beige clunker of a car. When she pulled up, I was sitting, hunched over on a parking spot stump, with my luggage in my lap and my backpack on my back. I took a deep breath as she got out of her car. The first thing she did was outstretch her arms, bury my head in her bosom, rub my back, and whisper in my ear, "It's okay. I promise it'll all work out. I love you, Branden. You're a remarkable person with a huge heart, and you're a beautiful friend to me. Don't you ever forget that."

We stood there in the middle of South Central LA, and she just let my tears run down her chest until they'd all run out. We got in the car and made our way toward LAX. Traffic had diminished, so we only had about twenty minutes together. I told her the story from the beginning, and she offered a listening ear and kept her right hand on my leg the entire time, occasionally rubbing it when I was struggling with the more emotional parts of the story. "Sorry I can't stay with you today. I feel terrible leaving you on your own." I explained that my mom and brother were on their way to visit with me. We hugged goodbye, I thanked her for her kindness, and I moped my way into the LAX terminal up to the counter. I explained that I missed my flight, and I handed the woman my driver's license.

"Branden James?" she asked.

"Yes, that's me."

"You're all set. I have you on standby for the eight thirty p.m. flight. I can't guarantee that you'll get on, but so far, your chances are good. I won't be able to let you through security or check you in until two hours before flight time, so just sit tight for a while." I nodded and went to find a seat in the terminal.

My parents are notoriously late. I think that falls on my dad, mostly. He's the type of person who decides to get in the shower when the rest of us are ready to get in the car. He's always been a procrastinator. Knowing I had some time to kill on my own before my family would arrive, I pulled out some schoolwork. I was craving a distraction from the fresh wound of my dad's abandonment. A music history paper was due the next day, and I had intense preparations for semester finals in the coming weeks.

But after some failed attempts, I realized I was unable to concentrate on schoolwork, so I went for a walk around the airport and picked up an airline magazine before returning to the departure area. My brother walked in eventually, and we had a short chat before we walked out to the car.

"Dad left you in Compton? Jeez, Branden. I'm honestly shocked that he would do that."

We shared an ironic giggle about it and proceeded toward my mom's van. At the time Shane was living at home and trying to find work after his exit from the navy. He had recently met my friend Renata from youth group, who he eventually married. In his youth, he'd made mistakes, as we all do. But I was left wondering how his offenses were somehow forgivable in my parents' eyes, while mine were not, even though mine were an innate part of who I was. He was living with them after all, and I'd just been thrown out of a car.

We jumped in my mom's van and I spent the rest of the day with her and my brother, talking about all sorts of subjects. On the subject of my sexuality, I stood my ground, never apologized, and refused to admit that I had done anything wrong. I also shared with my mom that I occasionally smoked marijuana, and she spoke out adamantly about it being a gateway drug. She reminded me that I needed to be careful. As usual, she dominated the conversation, with Shane and me hardly getting in a word edgewise.

For her part, she lodged complaints about the difficulty of living with our dad, reminisced about her time as a kid in Los Angeles, and gushed about Ashley and about her granddaughter, Isabella. When she restated her defense for my dad and his actions, I just rolled my eyes and said I disagreed and didn't want to discuss it with her.

"What he did was wrong, Mom. I don't care how he feels. If he truly loved his son, he wouldn't throw him out of a car in a dangerous neighborhood. I'm done with him." She just shook her head in disappointment and drifted to a new conversation. She didn't ask once about my personal life, about my relationship, nor did she make any further mention of my sexuality. We did exchange some views about the differences between living in San Francisco and Orange County. I defiantly told her how much more I enjoyed living in San Francisco, where the people were open-minded.

She asked me, "Have you ever heard the expression 'an open mind is like an open wound'?"

I told her I hadn't, but it sounded ridiculous to me, because that meant you were closing yourself off to so many life experiences and people with different viewpoints. I made haughty references to Jesus, saying, "When Jesus was on Earth, he never closed himself off to anyone. He embraced and forgave the sinners, he cared for the sick and the poor, and he welcomed the outcasts with open arms." Although I was more or less antireligion at that point, I still found it an effective argument to use biblical references as ammunition against her. I could only hope that it would make sense to my mother on some level, even if she would never admit it.

There were so many terms I grew up with in my household that are still part of my family's everyday vernacular: *God's will, God's plan, the will of the Lord, the power of the Holy Spirit, keeping the faith, what would Jesus do?* The list goes on and on. If we went into a secular home and rattled off these terms as often as we did at our house, we'd leave everyone in confusion. I suppose that's what faith is, though: having absolute belief in things that are intangible and unknown.

My mother found her faith genuinely: through a baptism on a beach in Orange County. I believe she was moved by what she thought was the Holy Spirit and had great conviction to pursue a personal relationship with Jesus. I don't fault her, nor anyone in my family, for that faith. I only wish they hadn't conformed to the more LGBTQ-intolerant positions of the church. The church put such strict expectations on them, which held them back, in my opinion. I have to hand it to my mom. She drove up from Orange County against her moral beliefs to spend the day with her son and comfort him. Even though her reception was chilly, I know how difficult it was for her to cater to both sides of a rift between my father and me. Despite all of the pain I felt that day, I never thought for a single moment that she didn't love me.

We finished lunch and still had plenty of time to waste until six thirty, so we decided to take a drive around the University of Southern California campus. Eventually I started getting antsy to get back home to San Francisco, so I asked if my mom would take me back to the airport. I told them a small fib: I needed to check in again with the airline to make sure I could get on the flight.

Concerned about my flight fate, my mom asked, "What will you do if you can't get on the flight?" I assured her the lady at the counter told me it wouldn't be an issue getting a standby seat tonight. I told her I'd call Christina and sleep at her place that night if there happened to be an issue. Truth was, I had no idea if Christina could come back to get me, but I knew I wasn't going back home into the lion's den where my father was. I'd just as soon sleep at the airport if all of my other options were exhausted.

We drove back to the airport and found ourselves without much else to talk about. My mom had been switching between Focus on the Family radio and worship music in the car throughout the day, which only contributed to my irritation. We arrived again at LAX, and they both got out of the car.

"'Bye, Branden, take care," Shane said as he gave me a handshake turned half hug. My mom came around to the curbside with a gift bag from the Christian bookstore and awkwardly hugged me goodbye. She handed me the bag.

"I brought you something that I hope will help you," she said. "Sorry, I know it's been a rough day." I thanked her for coming up to spend the day with me and put the gift bag in my backpack. "Are you going to be home for Christmas?" she asked.

I replied politely, "I don't think so. Not this year."

She pulled me in and gave me a bigger hug and shed a couple of tears. In a broken voice, she pressed her cheek against mine and said, "I love you, Branden."

I waved goodbye as they pulled away from the airport, got myself a standby pass, and proceeded through security. On the other side of the terminal, I opened my bag to grab some more homework, having forgotten about the gift she'd given me. Reaching into the paper bag, I pulled out a book entitled, *The Battle for Normality: A Guide for (Self-) Therapy for Homosexuality.* The tagline on the cover read, "Constructive help and support for men and women troubled by unwanted homosexual feelings and/or behavior." Although I was seething with anger when I saw this, I still opened the book and skimmed through the contents. I didn't see anything in the book that would ease my angst at that moment, so I threw it back in my bag and eventually stored it in a box of mementos I kept at home in San Francisco. I didn't understand how my mom could say she loved me and at the same time hand me a book that told me I was doing everything wrong. I wouldn't understand this for years to come.

CHAPTER
ELEVEN

jumped right back into school and seemed to excel the most at language diction and music history. Next to that was musicianship. Still, I made mistakes from time to time: so much so that my musicianship teacher, the well-known modern composer David Garner, took me aside and said, "I don't know how to say this except to just say it . . . When I'm conducting class exercises in sight reading and you sing along, you tend to make a lot of mistakes. I wouldn't normally bring this up, but your voice is so damned beautiful that most of the class goes with you, and then they end up learning things incorrectly. You could stand to study sight singing a little more. And perhaps in class, you could sing a little quieter?"

This could have bruised my ego, but I didn't mind constructive criticism, especially when it came from people I admired and respected. I understood completely. I reminded myself that I didn't come from a pedigree of classical music. I was only introduced to this game a few years previously, so rather than beat myself up for these mistakes, I decided to give myself a break. That was something I was rather proud of, actually. I'd never given myself a break before. Self-loathing has always and forever been my way of life.

As I continued to work at JohnFrank restaurant in the Castro, I found myself with a lot more cash at hand. It was a fruitful place to work, and combined with holiday singing gigs and church, I was minted for a student my age. None of this meant that I was financially responsible. My father was notoriously bad with finances, so he never passed on any financial guidance of any kind. I had credit card debt that I sometimes allowed to go late, and I even spent over $1,000 one day on a new wardrobe with my leftover student loan money, which was supposed to be allotted for living expenses. Oh, to think how stupid *that* was; I'm still paying off those student loans and will be for decades in the future.

One night after finishing work, I decided to walk up to the Café to meet my friend Chris for a drink or five. I left through the back entrance of the restaurant, walked around the corner, and headed up the south side of Market Street. I spotted a young, handsome guy crossing the street and walking in the same direction I was. We reached the corner at the same time, our eyes met, and we carried off in the same direction toward the heart of the Castro. With the same build and height, we were sharing the sidewalk and walking at the exact same pace. After about ten minutes of this, I decided to say hello to him.

"Hi, how are you?" I asked. "My name's Branden."

He turned his head, gave me a warm smile, and said, "Hi, I'm Jake. Nice to meet you." We continued to chat for another fifteen minutes or so and discovered that we were heading to the same bar. He happened to have just finished his shift at a restaurant nearby—a trendy supper club in town that featured DJs and live music. I'd never been in there because I knew it was pricey, but I'd heard amazing things about it.

Jake mentioned he was by himself that night, so I invited him to come and hang out with me and Chris. Unfortunately, Chris was a little cold to him, I think because he had a crush on me. But I was instantly drawn to Jake. He was just so adorable, and meek and mild at first meeting. Chris got the picture after a while and left the bar in frustration. Jake and I had several more drinks and moved onto the balcony, where we decided to have a heart-to-heart conversation about life and family. He was another former evangelical kid who had only recently moved to San Francisco himself. After just one conversation, I was completely infatuated with him. We stayed until last call at 1:35 a.m. and exchanged phone numbers. I promised I'd call him the next week and we could get together. I made no mention of my boyfriend, Michael.

I only lasted until Monday before I decided I had to see Jake again. I explained to Michael where we'd met, and he agreed to have him over. Jake was free midweek, and I invited him over to our place for dinner. The three of us had a lovely home-cooked meal and lots of wine with dinner. But he didn't stay very long—after dinner he made a quick exit. I was going round and round in my head, trying to figure out what I had done. Of course, I never realized how awkward it must've been to have a connection with a guy and then be invited to his house for dinner, only to find out that he had a boyfriend. The next afternoon, I got a phone call from Jake, and he apologized for escaping so quickly the night before.

I asked, "Are we going to see each other again?"

His reply sounded angry. "I don't think we should. You have a boyfriend. It was nice to meet you, but I need to go."

"Um. Oh, okay. I'm sorry if I offended you in some way."

Click. The phone went silent, and that was the last I heard from him.

The days grew closer to Christmas. My mom sent me several emails and left voice mails offering to buy my flight home. "I know things have been hard, Branden, but I really want my family all together at Christmastime."

Knowing how important this was to her, I accepted her peace offering and went home, despite the fact that I hadn't said a word to my dad, nor was I planning to. I made sure to be smart about it at least; I brought a buffer of foreign students home with me. Ingrid, the Norwegian violinist, and her devastatingly handsome cellist brother, Liam Olsen, had nowhere to go for Christmas. They desperately wanted to go home to Norway, where their parents were waiting, but they didn't see the point in paying all that money for just a few weeks home.

So I called my mom and asked if I could bring a Norwegian brother and sister home with me for the holidays. My parents were always open to accepting company of any kind, especially those who had nowhere to go. Despite their financial troubles, they always made room for those less fortunate than themselves. We had a wonderful time at Christmas. Ingrid and Liam made us feel like a truly happy family. Their energy was infectious, and we were all entertained simply by comparing Christmas traditions and learning basic Norwegian words. My dad and I got along and spoke as if nothing had ever happened. I suppose most of this was a show for my Scandinavian friends, but some of it also seemed genuine. God bless Ingrid. She always had a way of soothing any situation.

We stayed through the new year and then went back to a bitterly cold San Francisco. January had been a month of record low temperatures, and for three weeks before school resumed, we froze. The weather improved in February, and I was anticipating my senior recital. Our guidance counselors advised us to book the school performance hall well ahead of time, but for some reason I waited until the last minute, so for my senior recital, I could only get the small, classroom-like performance hall upstairs where my musical history classes were held.

I was in a daze at that time, working full-time, going to a therapist to try and heal the pain I was dealing with from my parental encounters. My therapist was a typical hippie woman who smelled of patchouli oil and often asked me about my dreams in our weekly sessions. She would prompt me to remember every detail of what happened in them and then relate the dreams to the broken relationship I had with my parents. I found these sessions abundantly helpful. And being the secular woman that she was, she guided me through a divorce of sorts with the church I'd grown up in.

Reestablishing regular communication with my mom, I told her about my therapy sessions, and she immediately voiced her opinion about how dangerous it was for me to be in therapy that wasn't faith-based. The antigay paraphernalia didn't stop coming, either. In the mail, I received DVDs to watch, articles to read, a Christian-based "scientific" magazine, newspaper clippings, and of course some very loving notes from my mom. My therapist told me to ignore them, so after opening them, I would toss them in a green storage bin that stood on a shelf above my closet.

Meanwhile, Michael and I were growing farther apart. I knew the end was in sight long before he did. My heart was unable to hold a place for him in it. He was busy preparing for his own recital and was constantly playing gigs for weddings, funerals, and parties in the Bay Area. My partner in crime, Chris, and I would hang out at various gay bars in the Castro, and often at a place called the Lion Pub, a gay bar with an older clientele that was in the base of a Victorian flat. I would also find myself at the Polk Street Theatre from time to time, where there were male strip shows. In retrospect, I think I was acting out as a rebuke to my parents. And I was also trying to fit in to a new gay culture. At the end of the day, I was just a twenty-one-year-old boy with senioritis and a party streak. Luckily, I refused to let any of my extracurricular activities affect my singing or my academics.

March rolled around, and it was unusually sunny. We were all reveling in the warm weather, going to the beach and spending time outside in the parks. Ingrid and I would ride our bikes around various parts of the city. She would always scold me because I never wanted to wear a helmet. I was too vain and didn't want to mess up my hair. You'd think after all of my accidents as a kid, I might have learned a lesson.

On a weekend in the middle of the month, I was preparing for a busy week ahead. I was scheduled to work Friday night, perform at a special event during the day on Saturday, as well as night shifts all weekend at JohnFrank. Not to mention I had to make an eight a.m. call for two services for my church job on Sunday morning. On early Saturday evening, I was in the back of the kitchen at JohnFrank helping to run food out to the various tables in the restaurant, when the manager/owner, Frank, came up to me.

"Branden, there's a phone call from someone named Michael. He says it's an emergency."

I rushed to the phone, took a deep breath, and said, "Hello?"

"Branden, something terrible has happened." He choked up.

"What? What, Michael!"

After a pause he said, "Ingrid has been in a bike accident. She's at the hospital and she's in surgery right now, but the doctors don't think she's going to make it."

I put the phone down and stepped away from the host stand and clutched the wall behind me. I was seeing black spots and thought for sure I was going to faint. I just stared at the ground for a few seconds.

Daria, the hostess, said, "Branden? Are you still on the phone? Is everything okay?" I didn't acknowledge her; I just grabbed the phone out of her hand.

"Where are you?" I asked.

"I'm here at the hospital, too."

I screamed at him, "What? Why didn't you call me earlier?"

Many restaurant patrons who were sipping on fruit-infused vodka martinis at the bar or enjoying their steaks and salads immediately stopped their conversations and stared at me. Michael went on.

"I didn't want to bother you at work until we got an

update from the doctors. Branden, I think you need to come down here. Do you want me to pick you up?"

"No. You stay there, I'll take a taxi and be there as soon as I can."

I ran to the back of the kitchen where Frank was and told him what had happened. Without so much as giving it a second thought, he said, "Go, Branden. Go be with your friends." I quickly turned in all the cash and credit card receipts I had collected thus far. "Don't worry about this. I'll take care of the paperwork and make sure you get your money for tonight."

I dashed back into the break room where the lockers were, pulled out my backpack, and ran out of the restaurant to the corner of Church and Sanchez to hail a cab. I spotted a taxi within seconds, flung open the door, gave the address, and yelled at the driver, "Please hurry. It's an emergency."

It took about thirty-five minutes in Saturday-night traffic to reach the hospital, which was clear on the other side of town. When I arrived in the ER, there were more than thirty students and a few teachers there, all with expressions of horror on their faces. Michael greeted me and gave me a hug and a kiss. A couple of other friends came over, and we embraced and said a few words to each other.

My friend Katy filled me in. "She was riding her bike up at the top of the Sunset. Apparently, a man opened his car door right as she was riding past him and she didn't see him. She flew over her handlebars and landed on her head."

I shook my head in disbelief. "But she was wearing her helmet—she should be fine. She always wears her helmet!"

Katy just looked at me, makeup and tears streaming down her face, and shook her head from side to side. Ingrid *wasn't* wearing her helmet that day. I laid my head against the wall and closed my eyes for a few seconds. When I opened them, Michael was sitting next to me with his hand on my leg.

"Ingrid's parents are flying here from Norway. The school called them, and they got on the next plane. They're not set to arrive until tomorrow evening." Her brother, Liam, was there, eyes red and cheeks blotchy. I went up and gave him a big hug, and he just melted in my arms.

We waited there for four hours with no room to sit. Many of us had found comfort in lying on the floor holding each other, telling stories about Ingrid, and some even took to leading prayers. The others waiting in the ER room were clued into what was going on, and some offered a few words of comfort. Eventually the surgeon walked into the waiting room. Several of us stood up immediately when he entered. The other students parted for us and her brother, Liam; we *were* her closest friends, after all. Liam was stone-faced, looking exhausted and defeated.

"Hello, everybody. If you can, I would like you all to sit down. Just find some space on the floor, wherever you can. Is everybody comfortable?" Michael and I held on to each other. "We just finished our recovery attempt eight minutes after midnight, but unfortunately, we were unable to save her."

There was audible moaning and shrieking coming from every corner of the waiting room. Her brother and Michael and I all held each other and just started to wail.

The doctor raised his voice. "I've been in regular communication with her parents from the flight. They have requested us to keep her on a breathing apparatus until they arrive tomorrow evening. Visiting hours are now over, but given the nature of this incident, I'm having my nurses prepare her for a viewing, if any of you would like to see her and say your last goodbyes. It should just be a few more minutes. I'll have someone come out and get you two by two when she's ready. Again, I'm very sorry. We did absolutely everything we could." He paused for a minute and looked up at the ceiling. "Please note one more thing. Ingrid does not look anything like she did before she came into the hospital. Many of you might be shocked to see her in the state she's in. I would advise you not to go in if you don't think you can handle it."

Brittany, the cellist behind us, said, "I'm going to say goodbye, guys. I don't want to remember Ingrid like that."

"I'm going to go with her," said another girl. Ten or so people left the hospital, and the rest of us sat on the ground, crying and hugging each other and grieving.

About thirty minutes passed before a nurse with a tender face came into the waiting room. "Ingrid is prepared, and you can go in and see her now. But you must only go two by two. You each have ten minutes to visit with her."

Her brother, Liam, started to walk toward the waiting room. Michael looked over at me, and I motioned for him to go into the room, too. I needed a minute to collect myself. About thirty minutes later, I went in with Katy. We were shocked at the state of her. She had been bandaged all around her head and had a huge breathing tube in her mouth that was breathing for her. There was dried blood around her nose and blackened eyes, and she lay covered on a hospital bed. It was clear that she had already passed, because there was no heart monitor, nor an IV drip, only an artificial breathing machine to keep up appearances. Katy and I said a few words to Ingrid out loud, and then she asked me to join her in a prayer. We left the room in tearful silence, and Michael and Liam and I went back to our house so Liam could sleep that night in our spare room. We drank some wine and told humorous stories about his sister in between fits of whimpering and sniffling. The mood was lighter as we all stumbled off to bed a bit tipsy.

The next day was a Sunday. I called in sick to my church job that morning and my restaurant job as well. Everyone understood. No one expects to hear that a twenty-two-year-old girl passed away in a tragic accident. Liam slept in until around noon that day, and I greeted him with a hearty American breakfast. He and Michael went back to the hospital because he wanted to spend some more time with his sister. I stayed around the house and just lay on the couch, as if I were trapped, unable to do anything for myself.

Needing some comfort, I called Maya in Switzerland and also called my mom. My parents were devastated by the accident and asked about when the memorial service might be, and I said I'd let them know as soon as I heard anything. Later that night, the boys went to pick up Ingrid's family from the airport and took them straight to the hospital. I met them there, and the six of us huddled around our lifeless friend, sister, and daughter as the breathing apparatus kept up the illusion that she was alive for just a few more minutes.

A priest came in to bless and pray over Ingrid and then prayed with all of us. Michael and I said our goodbyes and gave Ingrid a kiss on her cold, pale right hand. We left her family to share their final hours with her before they authorized the termination of her respirator. Her parents were stricken with anguish and confusion and astonishment. Aside from the few senior relatives in my family, I had never lost anyone close to me. There is nothing more heartbreaking than the reality of burying a child before their parent dies. It's just not part of what the Western world considers to be the natural order. Michael and I left the hospital on our own, and the Olsen family made their way with their luggage to a nearby hotel.

A somber tone struck the entire school the next day. There were students hugging each other and crying together. The school counselor's office was booked all day with grief-management appointments, and the student lounge had turned into a shrine of candles, flowers, hand-written cards, and photos to memorialize the girl who had touched us all with her giant heart. In the middle of the day, the dean of the school broadcast over an intercom system that I never knew existed, announcing that Ingrid's memorial service would be on Friday. Her family arrived that afternoon and sat in the student lounge and visited with students who wanted to share stories of how their daughter had impacted their lives.

The next morning, I got a phone call on the orange Nokia cell phone that I'd recently acquired. It was the dean of the school, Susan. I greeted her grimly.

"I have to go and collect Ingrid's bicycle and her clothes from the police station," she said. "Her parents would like to see them, and I was hoping you could come with me."

I of course said yes, and we left for the station following my afternoon classes the next day. I wasn't prepared for the sight of her torn, bloody clothing, which they had cut away and ripped off her at the accident site. Nor was I ready to see the remains of her smashed bicycle. Vivid images of the moments before she was hit kept flashing through my head. *What was she thinking about? What was she looking at? How come none of us knew where she was or what she was doing that afternoon?*

I was a useless student that week; we all were. I canceled my voice lessons and spent most of my time by myself. Michael spent his time organizing a concert for the memorial service on Friday. Ingrid's favorite composer was the romantic-era Edvard Grieg. He still remains the most prominent Norwegian composer in history. His iconic piece called "The Holberg Suite" was scheduled to open the concert, and the plan was to leave the first violin chair of the orchestra open in her memory.

I was asked by the student organizers of the service if I would sing César Franck's "Panis Angelicus." I'd sung at my great-grandmother's funeral and my grandfather's as well. It was a terrible position to be in, singing at the funeral of a loved one. It's nearly impossible to sing and cry at the same time. In those occasions, I had to reach deep inside and put on a stoic face, detaching myself from the sight of my grieving grandmother, parents, aunts, uncles, and cousins. I had to save all of my grieving for after my performance if I was to honor them with integrity. It was no different at Ingrid's funeral. The only comfort about this memorial was that I was just one of many performers who were beholden to the same task.

The day of the memorial service arrived, and I attended the morning rehearsal along with everyone else who was slated to perform and speak. After I finished rehearsing, I walked out of Hellman Hall and into the student lounge.

Ingrid's family was sitting on the couches, where they'd been all week. This time they were wearing black. I looked toward the shrine and gasped when I saw my dad sitting on one of the lounges near the multiple flower arrangements. He hopped up and extended his arms toward me to give me a big hug. I hugged him back and let out a deep sigh of relief. I was supposed to call my parents and tell them when the memorial service was. I'd completely forgotten about the whole thing, but he'd still made it.

"Your mom wanted me to apologize that she's not here for you today. She just couldn't get away from work and needed to be at home for Ashley."

I looked straight into my dad's eyes. "It's okay. I understand. I'm glad you're here, Dad."

"Bub, you know I'd drive to New York City and back for you if I had to."

"I know you would, Dad," I said as I gave him another hug. He always used to say that to me, often interchanging the cities with places that I lived or places that I was visiting. It's always been his way of saying he'd do anything for me.

––––––––––

A few years after her death, I went back to Ingrid's birth-place in Norway, a fishing village that is surrounded by breathtaking fjords. Her parents invited me to sing a memorial concert in her honor at their local church. I prepared some of Edvard Grieg's beautiful art songs and sang them in the church she grew up in. I spent time in her bedroom, where everything was left in its place as she had last left it.

The loss of my dear friend Ingrid gave me my first adult epiphany about how valuable my loved ones were to me.

I realized that life is precious and that we must carefully cherish the relationships we have through the best and worst of times. She was the model of what I consider a Christian. Without an ounce of zealotry in her, she never passed judgment on me or Michael, nor did she force her beliefs or opinions on anyone. Ingrid never presumed that anyone else should follow her beliefs, yet she wore them proudly on her sleeve for all of us to see. She prayed for us and kept us close to her heart and looked out for all of her fellow human beings.

My mom refers to this resolve to choose love over everything else as *love at all costs*. My father's health had nearly taken him away from us a few years earlier, yet I still allowed my heart to be hardened by pain. But that's how stubborn we tend to be as humans. We often forget about the ways in which we're all the same, wherever we go. In that moment, when my dad and I embraced next to the breathtaking wall of flowers and flickering lights, erected out of an unfathomable tragedy, we understood that despite our differences, it was more important for us to love each other. His surprise visit was his way of proving to me that his love for me transcended the difference in our views. When it mattered most, he was there for me without caveat or condition. That is what true, unconditional love is.

CHAPTER
TWELVE

Things returned to normal fairly quickly. They had to. I was still in the middle of my final spring semester and starting to prepare senior projects that were due just before graduation. We were also rehearsing for the school opera, Count Ory, and I was playing the lead, navigating my way through a Rossini tenor role with incredibly demanding tessitura and countless arias filled with coloratura. The Olsen family flew Ingrid's body home, and we did what we could to move on from that horrifying experience. Michael and I continued to grow apart during this time. He was sleeping more in the living room on his futon, and I'd take the bed in the bedroom. I, meanwhile, continued to explore friendships outside my student body. I was graduating in the spring, and maybe it was also less painful for me if I disassociated from Ingrid's other friends.

Spending time in the Castro was like a Band-Aid for the void in my self-esteem. For instance, I was walking down the street one day after indulging in a dessert from Hot Cookie when a man with salt-and-pepper hair approached me. He asked, "Have you ever done any modeling?" And this wasn't the first time I'd been asked that question. A few months previously, a man had asked me if I'd ever consider doing gay porn. I immediately declined *that* proposal and just assumed that this was going to be the same.

I asserted, "No, thanks. I'm good," and I just kept walking.

"Wait, wait!" insisted the man. "You'd be on the cover of a magazine, and it pays $750. No nudity." My ears perked up, and I turned around in a flash. Now he had my attention. "The shoot is this Saturday, and you'll be paid as soon as you're finished. It's for a publication called *XY* magazine, and I was hoping I could feature you in the gay jocks issue."

I laughed out loud, recalling how I'd quit football directly after hell week. The man who was wooing me was not entertained.

"What's so funny?" he asked.

I kept laughing and finally composed myself enough to tell him, "I'm terrible at sports and I haven't played them in years." I just found it hysterical that suddenly the music geek opera singer was wanted for a stint as a sports jock.

I followed him through an alley and then up a set of stairs in the back of a Victorian house on Eighteenth Street to his office, where I signed a contract with his assistant and got all of the location details for the weekend shoot. I needed the money, and despite the back alley, the whole situation seemed rather harmless. On the day of the shoot, the photographer must have been briefed about my inexperience with sports, because in every shot, I was asked to struggle to do a pushup, get tackled by the other boys on the muddy football field, miss the hoop in my basketball debut, and feign distress as I fell on the floor over and over again. I suppose it was meant to look satirical to see my mug on the cover of the magazine, holding a football with the caption, "Caution: Gay Jocks." The readers were in for a surprise when I turned into the comic relief of the publication.

When the magazine came out, I had a good laugh about it and became a celebrity around the Castro. The publication was everywhere, and people in the Castro kept approaching me to confirm that I was indeed the guy with the football in his arm. *XY* magazine even made it down to Southern California, where my brother's wife's sister spotted it at a bookstore. She immediately told my mom, who both called me and emailed me to confirm the allegations.

I vehemently denied her claims. I justified my lying because that magazine was none of their business, nor did I owe it to them to tell them about it. It was my prerogative. The common cycle that started at home so many years ago continued, and my mom kept on confronting me with business about my life well after I'd moved out of the house. She never wanted to give me the opportunity to figure out my sexuality on my own, I thought. She was just going to keep telling me how much I'd embarrassed and disappointed them.

But now, I was absolved of any guilt about it. I had an extra $750 in my pocket, a giant amount of attention, and something I could brag about, at least to my understanding friends.

I found this ambush-style confrontation from my parents to be exceptionally distressing, and it would only fill me with more rebellion. It didn't seem like they were willing to allow me to be my own person. I had earned the right to be who I was at this point, but they were unrelenting in their judgment. I felt defiant toward them and, more so, toward the hypocrisy of the church they raised us in. We were taught that we were all born into sin, but that with Jesus as our savior, we were exonerated. So why did they insist on telling me how wrong I was, if I was already forgiven in God's eyes?

It would be different if I were actually *doing* things that were wrong. But I wasn't wrong: I was just *me*. Granted, I did plenty of other things that would raise flags for any parent, but I never shared any of that behavior with them. Their central focus was on my sexuality—that was my sin and my wrongdoing in their eyes. But by now, there was nothing that could convince me that their meddling ways were justified. At the time, they were attending support groups with other Christian parents of LGBTQ children. I'd still receive a book or a DVD occasionally, explaining from the church's perspective why I was living in sin. Sometimes I'd glance over the material, but often I'd just throw it straight in the trash. Although I felt guilty at times for ignoring their guidance, I knew it was the only way I could begin to find peace within myself. What I had yet to discover was just how deep my guilt and shame ran through me.

———

After a busy Friday night at my restaurant job, I finished my shift and walked out of the back of the restaurant, and there was Jake, standing on the same corner I'd met him at months ago. I hadn't seen him or even thought about him in ages. He appeared to be waiting for me. I crossed the street and we both blushed a bit, stifling smiles that were difficult to control.

"Hey," he said. The look on his face was smug but had a peculiar sense of humility about it. "Wanna grab a drink?" I wasn't sure if I should do this, but I acquiesced.

"Yeah, sure. Why not?" I replied with a smile. We walked up Market Street and caught up on life for about fifteen minutes. By the time we got to the Café, I knew without a doubt that I was going to fall deeply and madly in love with this guy.

"I'm really sorry about the way we left things," he said as he leaned in close to my ear. "I got scared."

The truth was, I didn't care how we'd left things—I was just excited to see him again. We had an electrifying evening together and closed down the bar once again. I caught a taxi home, but not before making plans to see him again on Sunday. We both had the day off, and he wanted to take me to his favorite Mexican restaurant. I agreed, but only on one condition.

"Let's have 'honest day,'" I said.

He laughed. "What are you talking about?"

"Well, when we first met, I didn't tell you about my boyfriend, and we didn't see each other for months. I don't want that to happen again." He nodded, and we made a plan for Sunday and parted ways. Michael wasn't happy when I told him that I was going to hang out with Jake, but it didn't stop me from going.

The next morning at eight a.m., the phone rang at home. "Hello, Branden! It's René from Switzerland." I was shocked to hear from him.

"Oh, hi, René! How are you?"

His tone was enthusiastic—it was five p.m. at that point in Switzerland, which most likely meant he'd had a couple of drinks. "I know you're still in school, and you said last year that you wouldn't be able to return to Interlaken this year, but we're having a hell of a time finding another tenor. Any chance you could pull some strings and come out? I can go with three singers and stretch for another two weeks if that would help you."

The proposal was enticing. If I went back to Europe again, I could move out of my place and live rent-free for four months while I figured out what I wanted to do next. I hadn't applied for any graduate schools, except for the conservatory, so I could always come back and go straight into school if I wanted to. It was also the perfect excuse to cut things off with Michael. I was terrible at conflict and had been avoiding breaking up with him for quite a long time.

But then again, I now had Jake to consider. We'd just found each other, and already, the thought of him gave me butterflies in my stomach.

"Give me a few days to get back to you. I'd need to speak to everyone at school again. What's the latest you'd need me there?"

"Ideally, I'd like you here by May 1, but I could make it work without you until May 5. Let me know what you think—and please, call me collect. I don't want to waste your money."

I didn't know what to do. Part of me just wanted to get the hell out of there and run away from everything. The other part of me wanted to stay and see how things transpired with Jake. I emailed Maya about it, and she was thrilled at the idea that maybe I'd be coming back to CH, as we called it—CH was the country abbreviation for Switzerland.

I had been kind of lonely when I was there the first time, but another easy, paid gig in the beautiful Alps sounded much more enticing than working thirty-five hours a week at a restaurant with a boyfriend at home whom I didn't know how to let go of. I decided a break from life was exactly what I needed.

I quickly organized everything with my teachers, and they were just as understanding as last time. My opera teacher said, "It wouldn't be very responsible of us to hold you back from paid work." She graciously released me from performing my final opera scenes of my undergrad degree. Of course, all of these early exits meant that I would not walk with my graduating class, but the idea didn't bother me at all.

Suddenly, everything moved into hyperspeed. I had final exams to take early, the opera was about to open, and I had to organize my trip. Michael was just as resistant as the previous year when I told him I was leaving again, but he *did* allow me to keep my things in the apartment and saved me the trouble of moving all of my stuff. I never stopped seeing Jake, even though I knew nothing was guaranteed.

During dress rehearsal week for *Count Ory*, I was approached at school by a man who introduced himself as Christopher John. Immediately I thought of the age-old saying, "Never trust anyone with two first names." With that in mind, I wonder what people think when they hear my name, Branden James. Christopher said he was a voice teacher in New York City and had sat in on some of my dress rehearsal for *Count Ory*. "You have an absolutely magnificent facility, and I believe with the right instruction, you could really have a giant career in opera if you wanted it." I didn't know whether he was peddling magic potions or telling me the truth. Christopher was a man with a high-pitched tenor voice and a build that resembled the late, great Luciano Pavarotti.

"I came out here with another tenor student of mine who's interested in studying here. Is it a good school? Have you enjoyed your time here?" he asked. I didn't have one negative thing to say about the San Francisco Conservatory. I loved each and every second of it, and I told him so. He said, "I know you're busy wrapping up the year, but I'm here for another five days and would love to give you a complimentary voice lesson, if you're up for it."

I was a little wary at first, but after some consideration, this opportunity felt legitimate, so I took him up on his offer and reserved some time in a rehearsal room to meet Christopher for a voice lesson. We had an inspiring lesson that transformed the way I thought about singing.

"Branden, I'm absolutely ecstatic about the work we could accomplish together. You have mega, mega talent."

"Um, Wow. Thank you," I said shyly.

"I don't normally do this, but I have a proposal for you," he declared, folding his arms across his chest. "If you can get yourself to New York, I'll put you on scholarship for one year. We'll need to meet at least two to three times a week. We have a lot to accomplish."

We finished our lesson, and I told Christopher that I would think seriously about it. I did love New York City, and I couldn't imagine having a better opportunity. Christopher told me that he didn't think I needed to spend the money on a master's degree. "Just come study a couple of years with me. I can set you up with a voice coach who can teach you all of the repertory. That's all you'll need."

I was so overwhelmed with tying everything up that I couldn't give him a solid decision at that moment. "Thanks, Christopher. Wow. I'm humbled that you'd ask me. Let me give it some thought over the summer, and I'll keep in touch with you." We parted ways. I left inspired and thrilled about the future. But I still had to get to Europe.

Jake and I said our goodbyes; Michael and I said our goodbyes. Mrs. Goetz my German teacher, thankfully allowed me to retake my final that I had failed, and I passed the second time with a C grade. It wasn't something I was proud of, but with all of the chaos that went on in the spring semester, my German course was the one I neglected the most. My teacher said she wasn't too worried and knew that I'd have the opportunity to expand my German abilities in the coming months in Switzerland. Every teacher at my school was so caring and nurturing, and I was blessed to have spent the past four years in that amazing environment.

On the flight to Europe, I reflected on the multifaceted time I'd had in school. There had been so many changes in my life, but I felt whole as a person and was already on my second paid gig abroad. This boded well for my singing future. That summer in Europe was just as amazing as the first one. I experimented with some drugs at late-night parties in the woods and around the lakeside. I tried cocaine but didn't care for it. Mushrooms, on the other hand, were an amazing experience. There was a shop in the capital city of Bern that would sell them legally. I was so connected to the nature that was around me when I was on a mushroom high. I would talk to trees and watch the mountains breathe. Epiphanies about various questions I had in life would come flooding to me. Mushrooms felt like a truth serum.

Jake and I kept in constant contact. I had given him permission to collect the black studio piano from Michael's apartment and move it to his place. Before I left town, Jake and I made a loose plan to visit my aunt's family homes in Turkey, in Istanbul and Bodrum. Wanting to be where all the action was, we also ended up taking ten days to go to Mykonos in Greece, making a couple nights' stop in Athens to check the Acropolis off our bucket list.

Our time in Greece was magical, and there was no shortage of partying. This was my first introduction to party drugs, which were easy to come by in the Greek nightclubs. I'd be lying if I said I didn't like them, and luckily I never felt addicted. I was too young to worry about massive hangovers, and the drugs made me a confident, outgoing person. It was an almost spiritual experience when the trance music at the beach clubs in Mykonos would crescendo and the effects of the pills and potions I'd taken would hit me. I met lifelong friends on that trip, some whom I still consider to be my best friends.

Despite the dangerous and reckless nature of partying at clubs with drug use, I don't have any regrets about doing it. Those were some of the best times I've had in my life. The drugs took all of my inhibitions away, and I had absolute permission to be myself without shame. That was something I'd never experienced before—living as myself without any shame, rather than hiding. That's part of the allure and the danger of drugs: the escapism that drugs can enable is intoxicating.

Our epic vacation came to an end, but not without its drama. We were robbed twice by swindlers in both Greece and Turkey. We were out of money and spent thirty-six hours in the Athens airport, which, at the time, had stray dogs and cats running around it. Maya ended up wiring us money, and we were able to make it back having only skipped a couple of meals. Jake flew back to San Francisco from Athens, and I had to go back to Switzerland for a couple of days before I flew back to the city myself.

Jake picked me up from the airport when I returned to San Francisco a few days later, and we went straight to a nightclub that was open from Friday until Monday. During our vacation, we'd decided that I would live with Jake for a while when I returned from Europe. I was shocked to find out when I settled in his apartment that Jake was planning to leave me with his roommates while he went to party in New Orleans for a week at a big event called Southern Decadence. But I had a profound love for him, and I was able to let go of my disappointment—or at least mask it with substances. At the time, in a frail state, clambering back from the trauma of broken self-esteem, I didn't know how to love myself and therefore kept turning to substances of one sort or another.

The following Monday, I went to my favorite spot, Baker Beach, to take some deep breaths and write in my journal. I was in this city that I knew so well, yet I had this strangely empty life on the other side of the hill, where I didn't feel I belonged. That weekend I was lost. I missed Switzerland, I missed Maya, I missed my family. Here I was, in my new boyfriend's house, with his three housemates I didn't know and who, I'm sure, didn't want me to be there.

My depression stoked the urge to experiment with some reckless behavior. I felt justified in letting off some steam— I'd worked hard during my school years and I deserved it,

I thought. Looking back, however, I believe most of that behavior was just another way to escape. There was a giant void in my life, and that void was my family.

When Jake returned, I forgave him instantaneously for leaving me alone, in part because I loved him blindly, and in part because I had no money and nowhere else to go. When the dust settled, I returned to my former job at JohnFrank restaurant. Jake and I made a firm decision to save some money and move to New York City. I wanted to pursue the voice lessons that Christopher John had so generously offered me.

In that six-month period following my return from Switzerland, I wasn't singing at all and instead was working a temp job for Wells Fargo along with the restaurant to save money for New York. I continued partying my face off on any given day of the week at all the San Francisco hotspots. As busy as I was, January came quickly. It was time to venture to the East Coast. The night before we left San Francisco, Jake and I decided to go take one last drive around the city and, most importantly, drive across to the Marin side of the Golden Gate Bridge to reminisce while taking in the night-lit skyline of the city. We'd often take drives through the Presidio of San Francisco and park ourselves at the top of the San Francisco National Cemetery. It was here that we would blast music from his SUV and watch the sunrise over the San Francisco Bay. I had acquired memories in every corner of the city. While many of these memories were collected during reckless adventures, I wouldn't change a single decision I made, because they shaped who I am today.

I never considered how big a transition it would be to move to the East Coast until I got there. The East and West

Coasts are two different worlds. Of course, the cost of living was astonishing, as was the poor quality of the produce and the lack of Mexican food in the year 2001. I was a softy, having grown up in California. People, I found, are more genuine—and therefore more direct and abrasive—in the Northeast. It took me a while to figure out that New Yorkers are not rude, they're just in a hurry. I quickly learned not to bother a New Yorker with questions while they were on their commute to or from work.

Jake and I drove all of our stuff to his parents' cat-filled house and left Jake's car there for his parents to sell before heading north to the Big Apple. The January day we moved into our Hell's Kitchen digs in Manhattan, it was fourteen degrees outside—quite a rude awakening for these California natives. We settled in, found restaurant jobs, and I started my opera studies with my new teacher. At my first voice lesson, Christopher John handed me a $500 check and said, "Here you go. This is for a new bed or futon for the two of you." And thus, we set in motion our new life in New York City.

CHAPTER THIRTEEN

Working in restaurants was a completely different animal on the East Coast. I'd had some damned good culinary training in San Francisco, but New York City restaurateurs required New York City experience on a résumé. It was difficult to convince hiring management that I was tough enough to handle the fast pace of New York. Using my charm, I was able to edge my way into a restaurant in our Hell's Kitchen neighborhood, only to leave a few months later for a new gig. Little by little, I discovered which restaurants offered the best benefits, which ones closed at reasonable hours, and which establishments required the least amount of work for the most amount of volume and, by translation, money.

The owners and management were often tyrannical in their delegation of busywork for servers in their downtime. We'd be called to work at three or four p.m. for a five or six p.m. opening. But NYC restaurants are often not busy until eight p.m. or later. In the downtime, certain restaurants would make us polish the brass and woodwork in the building or fold enough napkins to provide for a nuclear holocaust. I had never had to do this kind of busywork at JohnFrank.

Another difference was that the tips were often pooled among all of the waitstaff in New York restaurants. This had some advantages, in that we would all make the same amount of money each night, but not surprisingly, many took advantage of this system and let those of us who were harder workers pick up their slack. It felt unfair to be put in particularly busy sections of the restaurant because I was competent, only to take home a fraction of what I'd personally amassed in gratuity. Still, I loved the business and enjoyed the social aspect. Many years after leaving restaurant work behind, I discovered how much I'd inadvertently absorbed the work of the Michelin-star chefs I was in the presence of. My cooking skills came quite naturally, as did my presentation skills. To this day, I'd be hard-pressed to find something more relaxing than going to Whole Foods and spending too much money to cook all day and throw a dinner party the same evening. Cooking is like therapy to me, and I owe that in part to my restaurant days. I never thought I'd miss having access to a kitchen on my travels, or that I'd grow tired of someone else doing all the work for me, but I do.

Meanwhile, I was also learning about the New York audition scene. My first audition in the city was for Baz Luhrmann's *La Bohème*, which was to appear on Broadway. I got the call from Christopher John on our drive to NYC and launched into practice, singing Rodolfo's aria "Che Gelida Manina" on repeat in our rental car for the sixteen-hour drive. While I didn't get the part, I was proud to have been one of the last three men up for the role. The heartbreaking part was that Baz was in the room at nearly all of my auditions, and after that, I kept running into him in various parts of the city during their six-month run. It crushed me when I didn't get so much as an ensemble part for the show. That was the naive twenty-two-year-old in me, thinking that I could just walk in and nab a Broadway gig in my first audition. That rarely happens to anyone; almost everyone has to pay their dues.

Studying with Christopher John, meanwhile, was a stroke of wonder. He wasn't just a vocal technician, but also a therapist and a mentor who would show me hard love when I needed it. I had a penchant for sabotaging myself. Whether in the form of drinking heavily two days prior to an important performance or eating a bunch of dairy just before a vocal lesson, I would find a way to turn my gift into a burden. For the better part of six years, I studied with Christopher. His approach to teaching was transformational. He was the man who truly taught me how to sing like an opera singer. I enjoyed the journey New York City took me on as an artist, even if I wasn't the most dedicated one. I loved the hustle of auditioning. I worked hard and I played hard.

I flew from job to job in those early months in the city. I worked as a canvasser for AIDS Walk NYC, setting up advertising materials at the various shops and restaurants that were willing to display them. I even tried being a foot-fetish model at a bar in the Meatpacking District, which has since closed, called the Lure. Every Monday night had a different theme: beachwear, military gear, sports jocks. For beach week, the producers of the party brought in bags of sand, poured it over a stage, and set up a kiddie pool filled with water. I would sit on stage, in a lounge chair or splashing about in the pool, and various characters would come up to me and play with my feet. The rule was that they weren't allowed to touch above my knees. I was paid $200 and fed free drinks each time I did it, so the whole thing was a win for me.

Eventually I earned my first opera festival contract at the Chautauqua Opera Company in upstate New York. Jake took classes at a design school in the city in order to develop his design portfolio. He also worked in restaurants and, like me, he was eventually looked to as a leader in his position— we were both called upon to update training manuals and teach the ropes to the new incoming servers.

There was nothing more exhilarating than living out my twenties in NYC. It was a city made for someone my age to make new discoveries and new friendships, to make mistakes and get myself out of impossible situations. New York made me strong, because it both rewarded me and obstructed me at the same time. I dressed up like KISS with Jake and my friends for Halloween and roamed the streets of Chelsea, the East and West Villages, and Hell's Kitchen. I soaked up theater and live music and any new type of cuisine I could find. Sometimes I'd get gratification from simply getting from Brooklyn to the Upper West Side in the midst of a storm, a blackout, or a citywide crisis.

New York makes you a measured person, because the city does not afford you the luxury of making giant errors. When I made mistakes, I felt them for months afterward, and so I learned to make fewer of them. I also felt a much greater sense of community in New York than I have in any other city I've lived in. *Sex and the City* was in full swing when I lived in New York, and I was living out my best Carrie Bradshaw life. My first turn at living in the city was more a success in finding my authentic self than it was a success in my singing career. Sometimes that type of personal success is far more important than any career.

I never enjoyed playing the opera game. It was such a rigid industry, where your fate relied on perfection rather than expression. To combat my disdain for the professional version of my chosen field, I would go home and play through my favorite Broadway and pop songs. I continued to audition for both operatic and Broadway roles but never once thought about songwriting or singing pop music at the time.

Artists often find it difficult to put personal work out there. I couldn't dance or move to save my life, and I wasn't confident enough to act, although I did have some acting chops. I realized my acting ability when I debuted at Chautauqua Opera in Carlisle Floyd's Americana opera called *Susannah*. I played a postpubescent, troubled boy called Little Bat who was friends with Susannah, a young woman who lived in a Tennessee mountain town full of religious zealots. Surprising myself with my ability to interpret such a complex character, I became interested in acting and took some courses in both stage and screen acting. But my growth as an actor was stunted by my own lack of confidence. I continued to learn operatic roles with world-class instructors, only to sabotage myself when it came time for important auditions. An actor has to be vulnerable, and that old impulse to hide myself thwarted my ambitions.

Jake and I moved to various parts of the city, even living across from the rubble of the World Trade Center just a month after September 11. Our last two apartments were in the Brooklyn Heights area, which was full of Italian character and brownstone beauty. Waking up in such historic and picturesque neighborhoods was like living in a series of postcards. I was in awe of the urban beauty that surrounded me. But the contentment I had from living in Brooklyn still wasn't fulfilling enough to stay in New York long-term.

Meanwhile, I'd allowed myself to become infatuated with a stage manager on one of my shows, which put a giant wedge in my relationship with Jake. Jake determined he wanted to move back to California, and I wanted to move to Los Angeles, because I'd always wanted to live there as an adult. While I was completely on board with changing our scenery, I proposed something to Jake that would eventually tear us apart. Our relationship was plagued by the difficulties of separation and dishonesty, likely worsened by the shame I felt from my religious upbringing, but I thought our love for one another was perfect—that it could withstand what I wanted to propose. Having been in two back-to-back long-term relationships, I suggested to Jake that I wanted to remain with him but live in a separate apartment in Los Angeles. I was getting claustrophobic and wanted to spend part of my twenties being free and cultivating some more of my own identity. He didn't see this as a positive turn in our relationship, and this disagreement led to our breakup.

Our transition was tough. It was most convenient to live together, even after we'd split up: we were both in saving mode for big cross-country moves again. But there was a biting chill in our bed that we'd once shared with such affection. I felt like I was sleeping next to a stranger. We'd purposely sleep on the edges of our side of the bed in order to avoid an uncomfortable brush of a leg or an arm. And on occasion, we'd wake to find ourselves in fetal position, spooning each other. It was like a dagger in my heart when one of us would retract from the other and pull out of our temporary reunion.

Ultimately, we both felt like we'd wronged each other in different ways. They say relationships don't end until you actually stop having contact with your former loved one. I think there is some truth in that. Time heals everything, and so does distance. Again, the subconscious desire to self-sabotage anything that was good in my life made me do the most heinous things to myself and other people. Decisions I made were implemented as if my own self-hatred was pup-peteering my life.

After Jake and I split up, I went out to Los Angeles to sort out some accommodations and get an idea for what it was like to live there as a young adult. My memories of the LA basin were from my childhood, so I had no idea what it might be like to be a grown person in Hollywood. I was completely burned out from the operatic rat race in New York, and I decided to take a break from the business. While I was on my visit, I met another guy named Zachary one night, and when I returned to NYC, I couldn't get him off my mind. Eventually we connected and went on a few dates together. He followed me around the country a little while I was touring with a holiday show. Zachary was at a crossroads in his life as well and was contemplating going to St. Thomas in the US Virgin Islands for a while to reconfig-ure his life plans. His father had a house there that he could live in rent-free. He asked me if I wanted to join him, and I immediately said yes. I needed a break, too, and some time to figure out what I was going to do next.

Jake and I still had one task left before I could leave for St. Thomas. We divided all of our possessions, officially moved out of our place in New York, rented a U-Haul, and drove cross-country to San Francisco, where he would be moving. Our friendship was so strong that, despite the pain that enveloped both of us, we were able to enjoy that five-day journey. When I finally left him at the door of his friend's apartment in San Francisco, I walked away and let out a deep sigh of relief.

With my apartment taken care of and my relationship with Jake officially over, I journeyed down to St. Thomas and tried to create a relationship with Zachary. It turns out that we were too different, and I certainly wasn't ready to jump into anything serious again. I kept riding him about petty things—correcting his grammar, pointing out his mistakes. This drove him crazy, and eventually he took me down to a secluded beach and told me it was never going to work. I wasn't shocked by this outcome. This felt like a transition, not a destiny.

We agreed to be amicable and to stay on the island for three months together. We lived on a property that was situated just across from a jagged coast on an old plantation. I got a part-time job waiting tables at a hip little beachside café. During the day, I would go for runs and swim on the expansive beaches around the island. There was a revolving door of Zachary's family that would come and go from their island compound. His sister and her boyfriend Wookie camped under a bug net outside. They worked at a nearby organic farm and would often bring their friends over to party at night. I experimented with mushrooms, and would often sit around contemplating the meaning of life, occasionally talking to the rustling trees. Sometimes we'd gather in the ruins of the plantation and talk about the joys of living on such a remote island. The acoustics in the ruins were so live that I would occasionally break into some heroic tenor aria, such as "Pourquoi me réveiller," from *Werther* by Jules Massenet.

Marijuana was prevalent on the island, and I used it frequently. In that environment, I felt as if I was having a spiritual awakening of sorts, like I was connected to the earth. I could even see beings from other spiritual realms. Often, I would find comfortable places to sit in the path of the trade winds, where I would read and write in my journal. I found a great deal of guidance from a book called *If You Want to Write* by Brenda Ueland. Some might call this kind of soul-searching reckless, but to me it felt profound. I don't know. Maybe it was nothing and I was just in full stoner mode.

The months flew by, and Zachary was getting antsy to get back to the mainland. I was convinced I could have stayed there forever. It wasn't practical, though, so I left a few weeks after he did, having enjoyed one of the best times of my life. I moved in with my friends Mark and Bryan in Los Angeles and tried out various jobs, but I struggled with any career that didn't allow me to be who I was: a singer.

My journaling opened the door to songwriting, and I composed furiously. I connected with a talent manager through Craigslist, and within months of being in LA, I was rubbing shoulders with the creative team at Universal Music and recording experimental music with cutting edge hip-hop and R&B producers. They were interested in developing me into a classical-R&B crossover act. I was invited to attend lavish Hollywood parties with Usher, Pharrell, Nicki Minaj, and the like. My world had opened wide, and I recorded demos for some of my original songs and cowrote with Marc Gordon from the R&B vocal group LeVert. I was also asked to write songs for other artists in development at Universal Music.

Despite the windfall from the music world, none of it felt authentic. I wasn't comfortable telling my new contacts that I was gay for fear of them rejecting me. This was 2005, but Hollywood wasn't progressive in the least. Many of us were in the closet and dating men in secret, because gay men weren't considered marketable. "Don't tell them you're gay," one of my friends in the biz advised. "They'll look at you differently."

My acting manager at the time also turned out to be a complete shyster of a person. He'd hooked me up with a producer, and as a green, naive twenty-five-year-old, I agreed to front some money for a recording of a song the producer and I had written together. I went to his house, finalized the details, and laid down a scratch vocal in his studio. I wrote a check for $2,500, which was a lot of money for an artist my age to part with. Within a couple of weeks, I discovered the producer was in on a scheme with my manager and both had vanished off the map and changed their phone numbers. The producer was rumored to have moved to Atlanta, and I never saw or heard from him again.

Although I'd had legitimate interactions with major players in the music business, Hollywood had still found a way to bite me in the ass. The whole experience was disheartening, and I immediately sought employment at an establishment I knew was safe: the Los Angeles Opera. I set up an audition at the opera and was offered several shows in the chorus. Piquing their interest for other projects, I was selected as one of the singers for their outreach program, in which we'd tour around inner-city LA schools putting on one-act operas written by up-and-coming composers. I was back in the opera business in no time, and also back into waiting tables, this time at Ashton Kutcher's Pan-Asian restaurant, the Geisha House.

But on a personal level, I was still lost. I didn't know who I was as an artist or as a person. I had some amazing friendships, but outside that, my life was lonely. I would look forward to Sunday afternoons, when I would go to the Abbey after my church gig with a handful of Vicodin. Oftentimes I'd end up meeting others who had cocaine, and I would use the cocaine to perk up after a drowsy afternoon of day drinking so I could keep the party going into the evening. When it came time to sleep, I would take a Xanax. It was years before I discovered that mixing opiates like Vicodin, Percocet, and Darvocet with benzodiazepines such as Xanax and Valium can *actually* kill you. I was living on the edge and numbing the pain of the separation from my family and the void that Jake left in my life with whatever was in reach, completely unaware of how detrimental my behavior was to my health.

Jake had been to visit once or twice, and I'd gone north to see him in San Francisco as well. We couldn't seem to shake each other. Meanwhile, I also went on several dates with various guys I would meet while out at night or through friends.

Then, one night, I had a particular experience with someone I called a friend. I was housesitting for some long-time friends, and I threw a little party, where we swam in the pool and hot tub and enjoyed a festive summer evening. My friend stayed behind that night, and what started as something playful turned more serious than I'd intended. After our encounter, I had this immediate, gut feeling that I had been exposed to HIV. Perhaps I was just paranoid from the weed I'd smoked that night. I lay awake for hours next to him in bed, quietly panicking about the whole thing. The next morning, my friend stayed for breakfast, and we discussed what had happened.

"That was too close for comfort, to be honest," I said. He immediately apologized for being overly aggressive the night before and explained that he thought that's what I wanted.

I would often sabotage myself by being agreeable to any situation—it was a surefire way to convince myself that people liked me, or loved me, even. I was like a chameleon, changing my colors to match each new person in my path, which some who believe in astrology would say is a trait of a Gemini. I'm sure my Gemini characteristics have helped me adapt, but sometimes I took it too far. I would often go along with any situation, regardless of whether or not I felt safe and sure about it.

Having never been taught safer-sex practices—only told *not* to have sex and to save myself for marriage—I was lucky to have remained STI-free as long as I had. It wasn't practical advice for a parent to only tell their teenager, "Don't have sex," without also teaching them about safer sex. Most of us do what we want when we're teens, regardless of what our parents say. But my parents were of the mind-set that passing out condoms would only encourage kids to engage in sinful behavior. In my thinking, passing out condoms would prevent the spread of STIs when kids ended up exploring the inevitable. But I'm not a parent. So I cannot judge them for the advice they gave me—only comment on the fact that it didn't work for me.

My friend left after breakfast, but afterward, I couldn't stop thinking about when I'd first learned about HIV. When I was in high school, I was at home babysitting my sister and TBS was showing the film version of *And the Band Played On*, which is an iconic book about the HIV/AIDS crisis in the United States and beyond. I remember watching that movie and feeling absolutely devastated, but completely unable to understand why. But now I knew all too well the implications of contracting the virus.

After my scare about HIV, I realized I just wanted to be at home with my family. I was scheduled to teach some voice lessons at my parents' house in Orange County, so I decided to drive down and stay overnight with them that evening. The next morning I woke up achy and weak. I had a slight fever combined with intense chills, and I couldn't seem to warm up, despite it being a scorching day. I canceled my scheduled voice lessons and just lay helplessly on my parents' couch.

When my mom came home from work that afternoon and saw the state of me, she insisted I get checked out at an urgent care. She drove me to the ambulatory care center and sat with me for a couple of hours in the packed waiting room. I finally went into the doctor's office and got a basic examination, where I discovered that I was indeed running a fever. The glands in my throat and pelvis were swollen. After reviewing all of my symptoms, the doctor suggested that I go home and get lots of rest and drink an obscene amount of liquids. "There's nothing I can do for you," she said. "You have a viral infection and it will go away on its own. If it's not gone in forty-eight hours, please come back and see me, or go to an emergency room."

I left that day blanketed with relief. I slept peacefully for the rest of the afternoon and the entire night. When I woke up the next day, I was already much better, and I drove back to Los Angeles in time to make it to my evening job at the restaurant. But as the week progressed, my intuition wouldn't leave me alone about the HIV scare, and I decided to call a testing clinic to get some advice on what to do.

"When do you believe you were exposed to the virus?" the friendly man's voice asked from the other side of the phone.

"Um. I don't know if I was, to be honest. I just have this feeling in my stomach that I have it," I replied timidly.

"It's very common to have anxiety about contracting HIV. Let me ask you a few more questions: Have you had any unsafe sexual contact in the last couple of months?"

I tried to swallow the lump that was forming in my throat and answered, "Yes."

He assessed. "If you don't mind me asking, do you know if any of your sexual partners were HIV positive?"

"I'm not really sure," I explained.

While his tone was warm and supportive, the type of questioning reduced me to a grade school student who was facing a trip to the principal's office. The man asked me a few more questions and then said he thought it'd be best to come in for a test. "May I schedule an appointment for you?" he asked.

"Yeah. I guess." I agreed.

"When are you available? I have Friday at four p.m., and Monday or Tuesday next week at two p.m."

It took me a while to answer. I was flipping through my appointment diary and realized there was no convenient time to receive bad news. I suppose there never is a convenient time. If I took the Friday appointment, I'd have to go straight to work afterward, potentially trying to hide some terrible news while donning my faux-Gaultier red-and-white striped sweater and serving sushi to a bunch of Hollywood assholes. Next week would be even harder, because I was supposed to drive down to Orange County for Taco Tuesday with my parents.

"Excuse me. Sir, are you still there?" he asked.

"Yes. Sorry. I'm here." I made a rushed decision. "I'll take Friday at four p.m.," I responded, still uneasy.

"Great. Since this is an anonymous testing center, I'm going to give you a five-digit number. You will be asked for this number when you come in. Are you ready with a pen and paper?"

"Yes." I reached for the blue ballpoint pen that was lying haphazardly on my desk and wrote down the numbers he told me.

I hung up, took a deep breath, and immediately reached for the pipe on my bookshelf that had a fresh bowl filled with marijuana. I picked up a lighter, torched the bowl, and sucked in with all my might, as if I were doing some sort of pulmonary breath test. After a few seconds of inhaling, I coughed and coughed until my eyes watered. I lay on my bed, staring at the green walls I had painted when I moved in. My glance shifted over to my electronic piano and the makeshift recording studio I had set up. As I scanned across the room and saw the meager possessions I owned and the disheveled mess I lived in, I started to ask myself: *What have I done with my life? Look at me. I'm a broke stoner who calls himself a singer but can hardly make a living doing it.*

That was one of the most disappointing memories I have of myself as an adult. I felt like a gay cliché and a failure.

M y friend Larry would often take me to lavish lunches around Beverly Hills and Santa Monica. We'd have prime steaks or fancy Mexican food with several cocktails each. Many times, I would go to my restaurant job completely intoxicated. Larry, his husband, and I had a connection that was rare for friends who were ten years apart. They were like big kids in many ways, but also like father figures to me in times when I didn't otherwise have one to turn to. Our lunch transactions, which traditionally occurred on Fridays, were a perfect way to end the week. We'd enjoy our first cocktail on an empty stomach before gorging ourselves on food that was far too expensive for my budget. I was his "Friday friend," and he could count on me nearly every time he called.

Since my HIV test was on a Friday, I knew it'd be easy to prompt Larry to join me for lunch and then get him to play hooky for the rest of the afternoon. We had a delicious meal at Frida's in Beverly Hills and then went to the Abbey in West Hollywood for cocktails. While we were at the bar reminiscing over a tonic of Grey Goose vodka and sugar-free Red Bull, I told him what my afternoon plans were. Always loving and supportive, he said, "No worries. I'll be waiting here for you when you're finished."

The STI testing and counseling center in West Hollywood was a short five-minute walk from the Abbey. Slightly intoxicated, I walked into the clinic and approached the front desk. Two or three people in front of me were also checking in. There was a line of yellow tape with the words *stand here* etched into the floor, which was meant to provide privacy for those who were standing at the intake desk, explaining their purpose in the clinic.

The lighting was clinical, as one might expect, and the walls were adorned with hanging units filled with green pamphlets that each had different subjects on them: syphilis, gonorrhea, HIV, chlamydia, hepatitis C, HIV drug interactions, safer sex, etc. There were magazines, some outdated, scattered on the small tables, with titles such as *POZ* and *HIVplus*. I had been in similar places before. Still, with the inescapable hunch that this time I was going to receive unfavorable news, each piece of paper was like a dagger in my soul, a stain on my psyche. I hadn't even checked in yet, and I was traumatized.

When my feet reached the yellow line, panic overtook me. As the person in front of me finished his consultation, I approached the counter, where a nice man said, "Hello. Do you have an appointment?"

I replied quietly, as if everyone else in the room was hanging on my every word. "Um. Yes. Yes, I do." Struggling for words as usual, I couldn't say anything else.

The man prompted me again. "Did you bring the number with you that we gave you over the phone?"

"Yes. I have it." I said. I opened my BlackBerry and read the number off to him.

"Great," he said. "Here are the forms you'll need to fill out. Please try and answer them as truthfully as possible. Here is a plastic cup. When your number is called, you're going to need to go into the bathroom and pee in that cup. Not too much, just enough to fill it to the line. And please let a few drops of your urine fall into the toilet before you add it to the cup. When you finish in the bathroom, write your five-digit number on it and put it in the window box."

I sat for about twenty minutes in the waiting room and observed as people came out with various looks of despair and relief on their faces. Some were even in tears. I kept trying to focus on reading a magazine, but even that was jarring. The publications in front of me were filled with stories of triumph over trials—of people who were beating the odds and living longer than doctors expected. About every ten or so pages, there was an advertisement for a new drug that was available to HIV patients. The front covers of these magazines depicted a happy and healthy person, generally of the male species, and on the back were truncated lists of all the potential side effects that came with taking the advertised medications: nausea, vomiting, diarrhea, depression, bone density loss, facial wasting, weight loss, fatigue, liver failure, kidney failure, hysteria, and death.

As a gay man growing up in a heterosexual society, somewhere along the way, I was conditioned and pressured to keep meticulous care of myself and to excel faster and reach higher than other people. I can only equate it to how society requires women to do the same work men do, only twice as fast, backward, wearing a pair of heels and bright lipstick. Beauty seemed like a requirement at that point in my life, and all I could see was a projection of me, ten years from the present, with a distended belly and severe facial wasting.

The door to the clinic opened and a heavyset woman appeared with a cheery face and bright smile. She called out, "Numbers 61247 and 61248. Come on back."

My hair raised on my arms as I slunk out of my chair and walked toward her, keeping my head down to avoid making eye contact with anyone else in the room. I could see out of my periphery that an older man in his fifties or sixties also lifted himself off his seat. We both made our way toward the door. His heavy breath grazed the back of my arms, and I was strangely attuned to the sound of his shuffling feet sliding across the linoleum floor.

"Who is number 61248?" the clinician asked. I couldn't seem to speak, so I raised my hand just to my ear level. She said, "Go ahead and take your cup into the restroom and give us your urine sample. Don't forget to write your number on the sample. When you're finished, put your cup in the window and go wait in room number three." I nodded, feeling slightly irritated, because I didn't want to be there.

I placed my urine sample on the two-way window and stared for a moment at the other four samples that were waiting to be sent off for examination. I wondered who had left those samples, what *they* were thinking. Were we all in the same boat, so to speak? It was hard to believe that, because I felt so severely alone. I washed my hands, left the bathroom, and went into exam room three, where I sat waiting as patiently as I could.

A few minutes passed, and a disheveled-looking man

came into the room. He had a long, ratty beard and wore a plaid shirt with a pocket protector filled with a few pens and pencils. He said it was a Los Angeles County requirement to survey me about my sexual history. He went into a barrage of questions about my sexual practices and my drug use that bordered on offensive. I understood why the inquisition was necessary, but it only deepened my guilt to hear the sound of my own voice answer such revealing questions. Maybe for the first time, I realized exactly what sort of behavior I'd been exhibiting.

After the sobering quiz, the woman who had summoned me into the examination area came back into the room with her phlebotomy kit. HIV testing had recently been reformed, and it was now possible to find out the results with a rapid test in fifteen minutes or so. It used to be that one would need to give a blood sample and have it sent to a lab for examination. These new tests weren't always one hundred percent accurate, but there was both comfort and distress in knowing that in just twenty minutes or so, I'd know my fate.

"Hello, there. I'm Leticia. Are you feeling okay, baby?" she asked, her tone motherly.

"Yeah, I'm okay," I responded, though I certainly wasn't.

"Just know that whatever happens, you're gonna be fine."

I nodded my head as she unwrapped a small needle and a tiny little tube. Stretching out a small, rubber mesh band, she wrapped it around my left arm and looked down at me. "You have good veins," she said. "You're like a dream come true." I giggled a bit. That's one compliment I never thought I'd hear. *You have good veins.*

"It's just going to be a small pinch. Are you ready?" I nodded and looked up at the fluorescent lights above my head. "You're all done, sweetheart. You can go and wait in the waiting room again, and someone will call you back in about twenty minutes or so."

"That's it?" I couldn't believe how quick it was.

I grabbed my small bag and went out to wait with the others. There were new faces in the waiting area, some in distress, others glued to their phones. One young guy, around my age, was tapping his leg at lightning speed, which seemed to irritate the others sitting around him. His left elbow was resting just above his knee and his left hand was on his chin, holding up his head. He was staring blankly at the wall in front of him and seemed to be in a trance.

I tried to play solitaire on my phone. I was looking for any distraction I could get. I checked the clock that was hanging above the reception area and noticed that twenty minutes had passed. My BlackBerry vibrated with a text from Larry. *Is everything okay?*

I replied, *Yes. Just waiting for results now.*

He texted again. *I love you.*

That's exactly what I wanted to hear, what I needed to hear. This is the sort of appointment you bring a loved one or family member to, but I was alone. I just wanted someone to hold my hand and tell me that everything was going to be fine.

All of us in that waiting area kept a close eye on the door to the exam rooms. Each time it swung open and a person appeared, we expected it to be a nurse calling one of us. A few minutes of playing solitaire gave me some reprieve from my own worries, but then the door creaked open and a voice rang out. "Six one two four eight, could you please come back?"

That was me. I closed my eyes and said a quick prayer in my head: *Lord, please let this not be HIV. I'm not ready for this.* I pulled myself off the chair and headed back to exam room three. The disheveled man came back in and shut the door behind him. He pulled a fresh piece of paper over the bed, and I sat down while he glanced through his files. He put his glasses on top of his head and pulled a pair of latex gloves from the dispenser by the sink. He placed his gloved hands on the sides of my neck. "How long have these glands been swollen for?"

"About two weeks," I replied.

"Is there anywhere else you're feeling pressure or pain?"

I mentally scanned my body for a few seconds and said, "Yes, in my groin. My lymph nodes are swollen down there, too."

He looked down at my abdomen and asked, "Could you please drop your pants for me?"

I followed his instructions, and he examined my glands. "Wow. These are really inflamed. You can pull your pants up now."

The man went back to the counter, removed his gloves, and grabbed his file folder. "Unfortunately, your test *did* come back positive for the HIV antibody."

I knew it. I knew it, I knew it, I knew it. What have I done? Branden, you're such a fucking idiot. How could you let this happen?

I hardly heard him as he kept speaking. "I'm sorry to have had to be the bearer of this news. As an examiner for the County of Los Angeles, I'm required by law to give you this packet of information as to what your next steps should be. The first thing we require is that you tell all of the sexual partners you've had in the last four to six months. After that, you need to go and see your doctor immediately and get a proper blood test done for confirmation." He kept droning on, but all I could hear was my fear. All I could see was that window into my dismal future—that image of my distended belly, my gaunt face.

The next moment I can recall, I was sitting alone on the examination bed. My tears yanked me out of the stupor I was in, and the kind phlebotomist appeared again. I was crying uncontrollably by now. Snot was dripping out of my nose, and every time I took a breath, my entire body would shake. She shut the door, walked over to me, handed me a few tissues, and pulled me in to embrace me like only my mother could. I stood there trembling with my shoulder buried in her bosom and just kept on wailing.

"You're gonna be fine, sweetie. You can do this. It's okay. I promise everything is gonna be just fine, hon."

I pulled away and started laughing again. "I'm sorry. I must look ridiculous."

"You are fine, hon. You're just fine. Take as long as you need."

Here I was slobbering all over a perfect stranger. She kept rubbing my back and handed me another tissue while I cleaned myself up and tried to pull myself together. She was an angel. She gave me one last hug and left the room while I took another few minutes to collect myself. I saw that it was going on five p.m., and I folded the HIV information packet in half, shoved it in my small bag, and barreled out of the office. I had to get back to Larry, and then I had to get to work by six p.m.

I texted Larry. *I need you.*

As I walked back to the Abbey, Larry texted me back. *Now you have me worried.*

I walked toward the bar where I'd left Larry, and he spotted me at the gated entrance. It was obvious from my face that I had bad news to bear. There was a portly guy sitting next to him at the bar.

"Brandi!" Larry said. "This is my client, Adrian. Adrian, this is Branden." Adrian put out his hand to shake mine, but I just walked right past him and sat on the other side of Larry. "Would you like something to drink?"

"Sure," I replied, and I just stared at the liquor bottles across the bar.

"Well, Adrian, it was great to catch up with you. I look forward to seeing you at the up-fronts." The two of them gave each other a hug, and Adrian left. Larry immediately turned around to me.

"Brandi, is everything okay?"

I started crying again. "No." I covered my face and told him the news.

He grabbed my shoulders and looked me straight in the eyes. "Look at me. Look at me!" he exclaimed the second time. "You are going to be just fine. You are strong, resilient, and handsome, and you're one of the smartest people I know. You can do this."

I wiped the tears away from my face and thanked him. My BlackBerry vibrated. It was a text from my mom. I ignored it.

"Thank you again for being here for me," I said. "I have to get going. I need to go to work."

"Fuck work," he said. "Come over to our house and have dinner with us."

"Really, you think I should miss work?"

"I think you need to take a couple of days to get your head around all of this. You need to be with people who love you. Come to our house and let's cook dinner together." I thought about it for a minute and decided he was right.

"I wanna be with Jake," I said. He nodded and rubbed my leg. Even though Jake and I had broken up, I needed the comfort of someone I knew I could rely on.

"I understand."

On the way home to pack a bag for San Francisco, I texted Jake and told him the news. I knew that he was at work, but he called me immediately anyway and cried with me on the phone. "Come up here," he suggested. After five years together, Jake and I were still connected and in love with each other. He had even come to visit me just a couple of weekends before. I drove home and started packing.

I had one important phone call to make, though, before I could get on the road. I had to call my general manager at the Geisha House and let him know I wasn't going to make it to work that weekend. He was a lovely man, a former baritone, and he favored me a bit at work, so I thought I could probably get through to him. But telling him that I just found out I was HIV positive seemed dangerous to me. Instead, I reluctantly told him that my father had had a seizure and was in the hospital. He was sympathetic and excused me from work that weekend. I had Monday and Tuesday off, so there was plenty of time for me to drive up to San Francisco.

I packed a small bag of clothing, brushed my teeth, and grabbed my bottle of Vicodin. Sometimes I would take four tablets of Vicodin at a time. The most dangerous part was that there were five hundred milligrams of acetamino-phen in each tablet, and that was quite harsh on the liver. I popped two and tossed them back with some water, grabbed my marijuana pipe and the dime bag sitting next to it, and went out the door. In my driver's seat, I packed a bowl, took a fresh hit, and started the car. It was rush hour, and I knew it would take me a while to get out of LA. Writing about this makes me shudder to realize how disconnected I was from reality in that moment. I'm ashamed I put others in harm's way with my reckless behavior, and I'm grateful that I didn't have an accident.

For the first hour or so, I listened to the Scissor Sisters and drove with the windows down and a smile on my face as if nothing had happened. The most frightening thing about drug abuse is that it *does* make you happier—up until a certain point. That's why so many get hooked on sub-stances. When I was high, I didn't care that there was traffic. I didn't notice my grief. I was just elated to be getting out of town to see Jake. I was buzzed at this point and feeling chatty, so I decided to call my friend Maya and tell her the news. We talked on the phone for an hour or so. She cried on the phone with me, too. Everyone cried.

I didn't quite know how to handle the news in that moment. I have never once thought that HIV would kill me, not in those days, and certainly not now. I think I was mostly disappointed in myself for having failed at being *gay*. I'd become a statistic. Instead of heeding every warn-ing about men's sexual health, I'd decided to forge my own path to destruction.

Part of that is true. I'll say it again: a lack of self-esteem will make you do the most unexpected things. But part of the problem had been ignorance. My sexual education came from my lone high school health class. Even when I learned about safer sex, my parents were upset and thought what I was learning in class was detrimental. They believed the information I was being fed was encouraging a life of destructive sexual behavior. Without much understanding about my sexuality, they had no basis on which to advise me. But it was clear to me now that I could have used a lot more education on the subject.

At the end of the day, I only had myself to blame—and blame I did. I often say that when I was diagnosed with HIV, it was as if I forced myself back into the closet. The shame that I carried with me about my sexuality combined with the stigma of the virus, and the pressure of living under the scrutiny of Hollywood was nothing I could ever prepare for.

fter my diagnosis, sometimes I would go to HIV support group meetings just to remind myself that I wasn't the only one going through this. Unfortunately, it always seemed like I was out of place. The stories that people shared were far more complicated than my journey had been.

I returned to LA Opera and worked as an office manager for an event-planning company, to which I also lent my musical talents. The owner of the company, who became a dear friend, made sure I worked just enough hours as a full-time employee so that I could have health insurance. I went to Kaiser Permanente for my HIV care and saw a middle-aged therapist who became another mother figure for me. She guided me and taught me about self-love. And during sessions of great frustration, she reminded me that I could benefit from years of deep therapy to address what I'd been through.

I dated another singer named David around this time. This was a period in HIV treatment when doctors advised their patients to wait to take medication until they needed it. I was one of those patients who would have my blood work monitored every month, but per my doctor's instructions, I would wait to take the medications. Unfortunately, this treatment plan did not do much to reduce the risk of spreading the virus.

Though I tried to be careful, I passed the HIV to David, which remains one of my biggest regrets in life. This caused me to panic, and I sought out various forms of therapy to deal with my grief: meditation, hypnosis, alcohol, marijuana, and more Vicodin. My body eventually broke out in warts, some of which were in my beard area and spread when I shaved. I had them cut off and burned off, which meant I had several slowly healing wounds on my face and on other parts of my body. I grew a goatee and tried to hide the scars as much as possible.

Even as I write this now, I wonder what you all are thinking of me. I assume, at the worst, you think I'm a monster, or maybe some of you realize how misguided I was. I don't know. I just hope you know that in my heart of hearts, I never intended to hurt anyone. Mal-intent is not in my nature as a person.

I was in denial about my new virus during this time. My friend Maya describes this period as the time when it seemed like I was running away from something. It's as if I were back in middle school, hiding in the library again, with the labels "guilt" and "shame" branded on my forehead. My late twenties were meant to be a time for emotional clarity and freedom from the confusion that had plagued me as an adolescent. However, I found myself far worse than I ever was in my formative years.

Ironically, as I struggled with my diagnosis, another

element of my life came into clearer focus. I eventually acquired another church job, and the choir was shortly thereafter invited to sing for Pope Benedict XVI's eightieth birthday at the Vatican. The momentous trip included a Mass celebrating his birthday and a reception on the rooftop patio of the papal apartment. During that trip, I started to find a new appreciation for religion in a way I'd never experienced before. Catholic traditions were a beautiful art form, filled with heavenly music, paintings, sculpture, and architecture. I was fond of the rite and ritual involved in the Catholic Mass, and I felt closer to God than I ever had in my life.

While I disagreed with many tenets of the church all through my adolescence, I was never able to let go of God. That's how I know that, for me, God is real. The Catholic Church felt much more laid-back to me than my evangelical upbringing. When I found a Catholic church back in Los Angeles, the organist and choir master were both gay, as were many of the men in the chorus. While homosexuality was not technically acceptable in Roman Catholicism, there was no trouble with any of us at this particular church in metro LA. And singing from the choir rows at the cathedral at Piazza San Marco in Venice and making glorious music in Rome at the Vatican will bring anyone closer to God. I held great respect for the ceremony of the Catholic Church, despite its controversial history. Around that time, it all became clear: faith and spirituality is a personal journey. The relationship I had with faith is between me and my God and no one else.

Through all of this, though, music never left me. I always had an open channel to it, regardless of how lonely or isolated I felt. My metaphysical self understood the value of music as therapy, even if I didn't fully grasp it in my current state of mind. So I dived into music as far as I could and self-recorded and released my first solo album, *Songs of Freedom and Inspiration*. My event-planning boss was so kind and supportive of my musical endeavors. He used to remind me all the time that my goal was to get to a place where I could play music full-time. He would tell me that I was happiest when I was working in music, and he was right. Using his business, he bought me a home recording studio. My album had a lot of songs that catered to his clients, but I put a few things on there that were original and others that I wanted to record for my own enjoyment. I was green. I didn't know what I was doing, but I made it work and successfully sold out of all one thousand copies I had made.

In September 2008, I met a contact through my church choir that led me to audition for the Twelve Tenors—a UK-based singing group. At my audition, I sang "Music of the Night" from *The Phantom of the Opera* so well, the casting director chased me out of my audition to ask me how old I was, and he offered me a job on the spot. I ended up touring with the group for almost two years and even recorded an album with them in London. My first stop on the tour was in Branson, Missouri. So I left Los Angeles, driving my car all the way to the middle of the Ozarks in southern Missouri.

I always describe my time in Branson as four months of my life I'll never get back. Even with a population of less than ten thousand at the time, more than one hundred shows and millions of visitors came through Branson. With a Bible theme park and live church broadcasts, evangelism was at the center of Branson's culture. Despite a healthy number of LGBTQ+ performers in its various shows, many of the people who lived there were filled with bigotry and hatred toward us, and we were often jeered at while walking down the street from our provided housing to the theater. Most of the guys in the Twelve Tenors weren't even LGBTQ—they were heterosexual and British—but the locals were threatened by their European style of dress, I suppose.

The producers of the show required us to speak in an Irish accent, and mine was rather useless. In order to perpetuate the myth, they asked if we'd kindly continue the gag offstage when we were seen out in town. Because it was quite exotic to have twelve "Irishmen" in the tiny Midwestern town, we had superfans who would come to our shows, sometimes up to eight times per week. They would always come through the CD signing lines for hugs, or just a hello. One woman would attend regularly and bring her baby, and she'd hold him up like he was Simba from *The Lion King*. Many teenage girls would come through and take photos with guys they fancied, and they'd get various items signed that they brought from home.

Despite its evangelical backdrop, Branson never ceased to fascinate me. Legendary entertainers such as Andy Williams, Shoji Tabuchi, and Charo, the comedienne and flamenco guitarist, were some of the town's biggest stars. One night, the twelve of us tenors decided to go into Andy Williams's restaurant Moon River Grill for a cocktail. Charo was there, holding court at the bar, and she eventually showed some of the other guys how to put lipstick on using only her breasts. I felt like I was living the fraternity experience I never got in college, having attended such a small school.

That little singing gig, which started in the Bible Belt in Missouri, ended up taking me all over the world to such far-reaching places as South Africa, New Zealand, Romania, and Scandinavia, with several tours in Europe. I acquired countless stories on my travels with these guys, but none of them could top the whacky behavior of one particular admirer. We were playing a three-week run of shows on a bus tour through small cities in Denmark, and there was one lady in particular who followed us to each place. She would stand up and scream and applaud the moment I walked on stage, whether I was singing or not. Her name was Marianne, and she was in her seventies. After a while, her enthusiasm was considered highly inappropriate, and she was banned from seeing the remainder of our Danish tour. When I learned she was barred from seeing our group, I contacted her and paid her a visit at a local restaurant. We had a lovely chat over a plate of meatballs and some Danish beer. She truly missed me so much that she burst into tears when she saw me.

In broken English, she told me how much I reminded her of her grandson. She asked if we could meet again before I moved on to Norway, and I obliged. Our second meeting was over a cocktail at a smoky bar, and she came dressed in a revealing outfit. Naïve as I was, I wasn't sure of her motivation until a few months later when I received a letter in the mail. She had planned a trip to Las Vegas for the two of us and even made hotel reservations at the Travel Lodge off the strip. In that letter, she asked for my hand in marriage and waxed lyrical about how excited she was to make sweet love to me after we were lawfully wed. Rather than let her down and tell her I was gay, I just fell silent. A few more letters came in the mail, but eventually Marianne caught the hint and stopped writing.

The job also reignited my love for performing. When one of our US tours finished on the East Coast, instead of driving my car back to Los Angeles, I drove north to New York City and moved back to Manhattan to pursue my musical dreams.

I didn't get off to a wonderful start. I fell ill with thrush shortly after moving back, and I officially started medications at the HIV clinic, per the suggestion of my doctor. By that time, my viral load was 175,000 and my T-cell count was down in the 200s. The first drug I took was in the combination antiretroviral therapy category. The most common side effects include headaches, inability to sleep, tiredness, fatigue, and physical instability. The more serious side effects can lead to an imbalance in blood levels, psychiatric fits, and toxicity to the liver.

I fell prey to trouble with sleeping, fatigue, and psychiatric symptoms. My depression became more severe than ever, and my moods were completely erratic. I was having trouble integrating with the other tenors on our European tours, and my partner at the time, Ross, was bearing the brunt of it all. The drug I was on was once sold as a street drug because of the euphoria it creates when taken at night. I experienced this a few times if I stayed awake too long, but it was never a high that I enjoyed. It's advised that you take it right before you go to sleep for this reason. It's also important to take it at a consistent hour. Being a performer and frequent traveler, it was impossible to take it at the same time every night. Sometimes it was ten p.m., other times it was four a.m. It just depended on the gig I was doing. Taking the drug erratically made it less effective, so said the doctors, but I never was consistent with the timing. Some of that could be attributed to my hunger for self-sabotage. The rest of it was just my creative self's general lack of organization.

It took me a couple of years to figure out that the medication was contributing to my mental instability, and eventually I changed prescriptions and got on some antidepressants. Somehow, while all of that was going on, I still managed to audition for the Metropolitan Opera chorus. I just decided to send my materials to them one day. I'd just returned that day to New York City from a corporate gig with the Twelve Tenors in Monte Carlo. I was jet-lagged, so after sending the materials, I went to the rooftop for a beer and a cigarette. Much to my surprise, I heard back from the Met that same afternoon, and they asked me if I was available to come in *the very next day* to audition for a full-time spot in the chorus. I went straight to the American Guild of Musical Artists website, where I saw that the base salary was over $100,000. I could not believe my eyes. I was living quasi-comfortably by the good graces of friends, but I'd never come close to breaking six figures.

Although I never got the position as full-time chorister, I did perform in nine productions there and was still able to take other outside gigs. Singing at the Metropolitan Opera was a dream come true for me. I felt like I had *made it* in my career. Sometimes I had to pinch myself because I'd go down to the canteen on a lunch break, and there was Plácido Domingo, James Levine, Renée Fleming, and Bryn Terfel sharing a meal and a chat together. It was like we all worked at the same factory, no matter what our rank was. And a factory it was.

The innards of the opera resembled a hospital: everything was stale and clinical looking, with fluorescent lights, scratched walls, and dirty linoleum floors. The rehearsal rooms had surprisingly terrible acoustics, and the building reeked of damp and mold. It was like nothing had been updated since it was built. All of the glitz and glamour of the opera house was reserved for the facade so the high-paying patrons could enjoy a proper experience. My first performance at the Met was a concert commemorating the 175th anniversary of the opera house. The day after the Sunday matinee, I was walking past a bodega when I saw my mug on the front page of *The New York Times* standing right next to Plácido Domingo, who was photographed warbling the famous tenor aria from Wagner's *Parsifal*. I stood there gobsmacked, beaming. And I thought, *I could die now and not have any regrets.*

I spent two years working at the Met, but even with all of those productions, I didn't put in enough time to be granted health insurance by my union. New York City has generous programs to assist those with autoimmune issues. My current medication sells for a retail price of $3,200 per month. That's one pill a day with a price tag of more than $100 per pill. I don't know many people who could afford that out of pocket, and those who are able would never stand for paying such a premium. My income as a full-time musician has aided me for many years, in that it allowed me to take advantage of those city programs. I've been lucky enough to be a part of social programs in New York, Los Angeles, Chicago, and Las Vegas.

However, living like this, by the seat of your pants, is traumatic. The AIDS Drug Assistance Program, or ADAP, only covers matters related to HIV/AIDS care. I knew that one day I'd need to have health insurance like a proper adult, but I had a preexisting condition. It wasn't until Obama's Affordable Care Act that I was able to be exempt from this problem in the United States' complicated health insurance programs. After that bill passed, I could finally be granted a health-insurance policy on a group basis without being questioned about my conditions.

One day while walking through the halls of the Met, I noticed a sign announcing auditions for a full-time tenor position in the chorus at Lyric Opera of Chicago. I knew nothing about Chicago but decided to audition on a whim, because it offered a competitive salary, full medical, dental, and a 401(k). Finally, I had stumbled across a big-boy job.

I immediately contacted my long-time voice teacher, Christopher John, and coached heavily with him in the weeks leading up to the audition. After two rounds of vocal examinations, I was awarded one of two full-time tenor positions in Chicago. When I received the news in May of 2010, I decided to pick up and leave New York within a few weeks. A long, hot summer was on its way, and I knew I'd prefer to jump in a lake in Chicago rather than hide in my bedroom with the blinds shut where the single air-conditioning unit was. New York is stifling in the summer, and there isn't a swimmable body of water anywhere in the vicinity that you can get to without long public transport and financial inconvenience. So, without ever having set foot in Chicago, I carefully mapped out a reasonable place to live and dived headfirst into the Windy City on Lake Michigan.

Chicago was a magnificent city to live in. Despite the

harsh winters, the quality of life was much higher than New York, and it was still reasonably priced in 2010. Like every metropolis in the United States, the cost of living has since risen significantly. I loved the Midwestern sensibility after having spent years on both the East and West Coasts. The skyline was one of the most brilliant sights I have ever seen in a city, and the whole region was overflowing with culture, museums, nightlife, and restaurants.

At work, I was the youngest full-time chorister by a good ten years, and because of this I was celebrated. I loved the job and the history of Lyric Opera of Chicago. Some of the world's biggest stars were mainstays at that house: Maria Callas, Luciano Pavarotti, Joan Sutherland, Leontyne Price, and José Carreras. Even winter was fascinating to me in Illinois. I'd experienced plenty of it in New York City, of course, but in Chicago, all of my intrigue was greatly magnified by the waves that would freeze on the beaches of Lake Michigan and the ponds that would freeze over and bring out ice skaters and revelers. I met lots of friends and some wonderful colleagues who guided me on how to live a life of fulfillment there. I quickly joined the Chicago culture, bought a bicycle, and rode it everywhere I could.

Our contracts at Lyric Opera only ran eight to nine months, so I was sometimes left scrambling for work in the summer or living on an unemployment wage. Still, I was thrilled to have great health insurance coverage year-round, a 401(k), and a respectable salary as a musician. I had arrived into adulthood.

Over my first winter holiday vacation, I went home to visit my family in Orange County. It was a nice visit, but I could only spend so much time at my parents' house; it was often full of people and it felt chaotic. I decided to escape to San Diego for a few days to ring in the new year with Jake, who was there visiting his best friend. While I was partying my face off in San Diego, I met a guy named Taylor who was in his early twenties. The kid had quick wit and could charm the pants off anyone. We connected immediately, and it wasn't long before we officially called each other boyfriends, albeit from afar.

I was now thirty-two, and it was the first time in my life I'd dated someone who was much younger than me. During my first summer hiatus from the opera, I decided that, rather than paying rent at my disruptive housemates' flat, I would save money and spend the summer with Taylor.

Taylor moved with me to Chicago later that summer and found a job within two days. We stayed with friends for a few weeks before finding our own modest apartment in Lincoln Park. Unfortunately, we didn't have to live together long before I discovered that we weren't a good match for each other. One night, after a particularly terrible fight, I was so angry that I packed a bag and went to stay with a colleague.

Much to my own dismay, I was only able to stay away from home for one day. I went back to our apartment and forgave him. I should have left him that day. But I didn't love myself enough to realize that I deserved to be in a relationship that brought me joy.

Our relationship didn't end then, but there were only fleeting moments of happiness during that time. I couldn't let go of the resentment I felt toward him. But at the same time, I was conscious of my fleeting youth; I thought I would never be able to find someone again. How preposterous, but that's the mental process I'd been going through since the time of my diagnosis. When you're given a diagnosis that can carry an expiration date, everything in your perspective changes. Many of my friends who were the same age were married and owned houses—they had at least achieved the perception of happiness and fulfillment. Those days seemed like they were decades away for me. But I was wrong.

CHAPTER
SIXTEEN

n 2013, when I went to my *America's Got Talent* audition,
I wanted my mom to be there with me. It would make
her so happy, and, despite our differences, it would be a
great comfort to me—she was still the biggest supporter of
my music.

The opera season was wrapping up at Lyric, and I was
about to go into rehearsals for their summer season production of Rodgers and Hammerstein's *Oklahoma!* The timing
for the show couldn't have been more perfect. My love for
singing in an opera chorus was waning. I was just about to
complete my third year at Lyric Opera of Chicago. Over
the near decade that I had been engaged in the operatic art
form, I'd noticed a bitterness among some of my older colleagues, who had spent years in the chorus. I think they felt
the same way I did—that they had more to offer as a singer
and had somehow settled into a job as a chorister, which was
convenient but not entirely satisfying. I had been looking
for ways to move beyond the chorus for some months.

Taylor and I had since moved to a beautiful building
in Lincoln Park in Chicago. We had a miniature pinscher

named Dolly, and she was the light of my life. Some people have kids to save their relationships; we got a dog. My mom had arrived just a day early to see me before the audition. I didn't want her there any earlier because I was delaying revealing my HIV status until the last possible minute.

My mom still knew nothing of my story, nothing of my personal health details. She only knew that I was auditioning. I don't think it ever occurred to her that I needed a story to go with my singing. She'd surely seen *American Idol* and *The Voice* and knew what the deal was, but she never asked me, "What is your story?" Leading up to the audition, I'd had my mind settled on openly talking about my HIV status on the show. It *was* an impactful part of my story—a hugely significant part of my life. But when my mom showed up in town, happily brainstorming songs for me to sing, regaling me with stories about my dad and sister, my resolve started to crack.

The day finally arrived for me to sing for my life. I'd only had a nap that night and felt devoid of energy. My anxiety levels continued to rise on the way to the theater because I was caught in a quandary. I wanted to tell my story—all of it. But my mom knew nothing about my having contracted HIV. And this was all aside from the fact that I had to sing Puccini's "Nessun Dorma" on less than five hours of sleep in front of an audience of thirty-five hundred people and A-list celebrities while a slew of cameras whirled around my face.

When I arrived at the theater, I learned that before I could sing for the judges—Heidi Klum, Howie Mandel, Howard Stern, and Mel B—I would need to do an interview. We were ushered back into a room filled with cameras and chairs for the family and friends who were there to support. They sat me down in a chair facing a set of large cameras, and a glamorously dressed woman with long brown hair sat across from me. In the end, she asked the same general questions I had come to expect from any reality competition. What's your talent? Where are you from? How old are you? Why are you here today? What makes your journey here unique?

I found the questions more difficult to answer with my mom sitting within earshot behind me. In a moment of clarity, I realized I didn't want to share my HIV status with the world. The last thing I wanted was for my mom to find out that way. She would have been devastated, and I didn't want to ambush her with the news, although I knew it would make great television. I decided I could never do that to anyone, let alone my mother; it felt far too calculating. Without that element of my story, though, I wasn't sure what to say. I reminded myself to be brave, and I just let it all out.

"I'm openly gay. My mom is here today. We have always had problems seeing eye to eye about my sexuality. I never had a chance to come out to her. She wrote a scathing letter to me when I was twenty years old and told me that she and our family disapproved of my lifestyle, and that I'd need to fix it before I was allowed home again."

I could sense my mom's energy shift behind me. I knew I was betraying her in a way, but I had to think of something else that was authentic and interesting that wasn't related to my HIV status. I ended up telling them everything: about the guilt and shame I felt growing up in a homophobic household, and the hurt I carried with me, even up to that very day. When all was said and done, I turned around and saw that there was mascara running down my mom's face. I knew I had hurt her. But I also knew today wasn't about her. It was about my journey, and the story was meant for others out there who could potentially relate. I tried to put a positive spin on the interview, reminding the interviewer that "My mom is here today because she loves me and supports me, and I love her as well. We're not quite as close as I'd like to be, but we're getting better every day. You know?"

After the interview finished, we were sent back to the holding area in the same chairs we'd sat in previously. My mom and I had a brief conversation about the things I'd said in the interview, and I apologized for sharing such personal details. Once again proving that her love for me was unconditional, she said, "I understand. I know your pain is real and that this is *your* journey." We hugged each other and sat in our chairs, just holding hands with one another.

Internally, I was conscious of a feeling of power brewing in me. I knew I might have hurt my chances of being on the show by not telling my whole story. But I also knew that I'd spent a lifetime allowing others' views and opinions to affect how I lived my life. In the process, I'd lost the essence of who I was. At that moment, I decided I wasn't going to make decisions based on who I thought other people wanted me to be—I would make decisions based on who *I* wanted to be.

Just minutes before it was my turn to go onstage and stand on the big red X, I went outside and practiced the scales my Chicago voice teacher had given me to prepare for the morning. These particular exercises were meant to clear some of the morning phlegm that can collect on your cords after a night's sleep. I took a few sips of water and said a prayer to God, as I normally do before any important performance or audition. I walked back in and saw my mom waving and whistling at me.

"Branden! They're looking for you. It's your turn!"

A producer was waiting for me. "Are you ready, Branden? I'm going to take you to the stage."

I looked at my mom, who gave me a nod of reassurance, and I followed the producer through the stage entrance of the theater. There were a few other acts who were also waiting in the wings, so there I was supposed to hold again. The waiting was agonizing. There's nothing more unsettling than letting your fears run away with you just before a mammoth test of talent like this. It still felt like another high-stakes audition—it just happened to also be in front of thousands of people this time. I buzzed my lips and trilled and hummed some excerpts from "Nessun Dorma" while I nervously paced backstage.

The production team had set up rows of dressing room mirrors, complete with vintage glamour lights, and small stools to sit on. They were stacked next to each other like cubicles in a corporate office. Some performers were sitting at their makeup stations, checking their appearance for the cameras. From backstage I could hear roars of both boos and cheers from the crowd, applause that ranged from rapturous to tepid, and the dreaded sound that no one wanted to hear that day: a judge or two pressing the red X button that meant they hated the act. I was getting more nervous by the minute, and I tucked myself farther back into the depths of the backstage area so I could sing at full volume and make sure that my voice would come out how I wanted it to. When I was more or less satisfied, I slid back out into the central waiting area.

I listened to the crowd and got lost in my own thoughts. I wasn't an *America's Got Talent* viewer, really. In fact, I'd never watched a full episode of the show before I was on it. It wasn't that I disliked the show—just that I hadn't paid much attention to it. This left me unfamiliar with what would happen when I got out there to sing.

"Branden, I'd like you to meet someone." It was the producer's voice. I turned away from staring at myself in the mirror, and Nick Cannon was standing there. My eyes widened. That was Nick Cannon, Mariah Carey's husband, right in front of me. The first thing I noticed were his Swarovski crystal–encrusted loafers.

"Hey, brother!" he exclaimed, giving me a high five. "Are you ready?"

He had an assistant next to him, a small woman who was whispering into his ear. "This is Branden James. He's a thirty-four-year-old opera singer from Chicago. He's going to sing 'Nessun Dorma.'"

"Whoa! Big song, dude!" Nick's brow furled as he watched my face. "You got this. You're gonna *slay* it." His demeanor was so casual and friendly. He was far cooler than my chubby, opera-singing self. I suppose that's what his allure was on the show—he was relatable. I just stared at him: his leather pants, patterned Gucci shirt, diamond earring and wedding band, and Rolex watch. *This guy is younger than I am, and he's already achieved all this money and fame. What am I doing here?*

It wasn't easy to block out the voices of doubt in my

head. But I remembered my mantra: *be bold, be brave*. It had gotten me this far; I had to keep believing in it.

"Just a few more minutes now," the producer said as we inched closer to the stage. From the stage-left wings, I could peer out and see the executive producers standing on the platform in front of the judges' table, speaking to the judges about this or that. I couldn't make out what they were saying.

"Are you ready?" the producer asked me.

"As ready as I'll ever be," I joked.

"All right, when I say go, you walk out to center stage and stand on the red X."

A tech person rushed a standing mic onto the stage, and I saw a stage manager watching the producer, with his right hand lifted in the air. As soon as he got the signal in his earpiece, he motioned to the producer from across the stage.

"Go ahead, Branden, it's time." She gently pushed me forward with the palm of her hand against the small of my back, and my shirt stuck to the sweat that was dripping down my sides. I walked on stage to rapturous applause and made it to the red X as instructed.

"Hallo," Heidi Klum greeted me in her German accent.

"*Hello!*" said Mel B, sizing me up with her eyes.

"And what is your name?" asked Howard Stern.

"Hello. I'm Branden James . . ." Howie Mandel motioned for me to get closer to the mic, as if he couldn't hear me. The judges' voices were incredibly faint, and it was hard to hear. I started over again. "My name is Branden James."

Howard Stern asked me what type of talent I had, and I said, "Well, I'm a tenor."

"An opera singer," said Howard Stern, seeming frustrated. Mel B muttered something I couldn't hear.

"Yes," I replied apologetically.

"Uh-oh. What makes you so special?" he asked. I wasn't expecting them to ask me questions that actually required thought. Luckily my adrenaline kicked in, and I was able to answer coherently.

"I think what makes me special is the passion with which I sing."

"Okay!" said Mel B, seeming enthusiastic about my answer.

"Why don't you take the stage and show us what you've got?" said Howard.

I took a deep breath, planted my feet firmly on the ground, and waited for the music track to start. There was about five seconds of silence that seemed to last five minutes. The audience was staring at me like I was a creature in a fishbowl at a freak show. The judges started to look around, and then suddenly the track started.

I only had a three-second intro before I had to sing my first phrase. "Nessun Dorma! Nessun Dorma!" I sang a bit louder than I should have. I carried on with the next phrase after a bar or two of instrumental music. *Phew! The first phrase is over*, I thought. I was shaking uncontrollably from the waist down, and only hoped the camera wasn't capturing my nerves.

I launched into the next phrase, and as soon as I began singing the melodic, triumphant line, the audience stood on their feet, cheering and roaring. I had to think hard in this next phrase, because I was meant to skip to the second verse of the song to finish it out. The track had been built especially to exceed no more than ninety seconds, per the rules of the competition.

I decided to sing the rest of the aria to the balcony instead of the judges. It wasn't often I had the opportunity to perform as a soloist for an audience of this size, so I was determined to enjoy it. Based on the audience reaction, I knew they were enjoying it as well. I crooned on, enjoying the rising energy of the crowd, and then came the big finish. I stretched my arms out as if to hug the entire audience. "Vincerò! Vincerò!" I finished my sustained high notes, oversinging just a tiny bit. I have a tendency to overcompensate when I'm nervous, and today was no different.

All four judges leaped to their feet, and the audience was chanting my name. "Branden! Branden! Branden! Branden!" I literally felt like a king. It was the most amazing rush I'd ever experienced. As a singer, I'd never received recognition like that before, and I was moved to tears. I had been through so many other auditions like this—it had always been my dream to be on this sort of television show. And, in that moment, my dreams were realized. The judges kept clapping. Howard Stern had this smile on his face that was giddy, almost like he was laughing with excitement. After a couple of minutes of cheering from the crowd, they quieted down and Howard spoke.

"Chicago knows talent, and I think this town just got really excited about your skill, Branden." Everyone cheered, and the judges went down the line to give me their feedback.

"I actually had goose pimples all over my body," Heidi gushed.

When it got to Howie, he asked, "Is your family here today?"

I replied with a beaming smile on my face. "Yes, my mother's here in the audience."

"Where is she?" Howie asked.

From the rafters of the second balcony, a piercing voice rang out, "I'm right here!" It was my mom screaming with all her might.

Heidi laughed, "She has a good voice, too!"

Because their voices were so faint, I essentially repeated the same thing: "Now you know where I got the loud voice from."

Howie got up out of his seat and spoke directly to my mom on the second tier. "Ma'am. You should be very proud. Not only is he incredibly passionate and a wonderful talent, he is going to inspire people beyond this show, beyond this building. You…have created a gem."

Howard corralled all the other judges together. "All right, well, it's time to vote. I have a good feeling about this. Heidi?" he asked.

"I love you. For me it's an absolute yes."

"Mel B?"

"Definite yes from me. Definite."

"Howie M?" asked Howard.

"America loves you. It's a yes!"

"We'll see you in Las Vegas."

I looked up at my mom and my partner Taylor and my friend Jeremy in the crowd. My great-aunt Lily and two cousins were sitting next to them, and I blew them all a kiss. I beamed and waved at the audience and then made my way offstage. Nick Cannon and a crew of cameras were waiting there.

"Hey, man! Congrats!" he said, nearly shaking my

hand off. "How's it feel?" My eyes welled up with tears—I couldn't help myself. "Why are you crying?" he asked.

"I've just been given an opportunity I never expected, so . . ."

Nick gave me a big hug and said, "You deserve it, man. I'm so proud of you."

That day, I was truly proud of myself, too.

When I left the stage that day in Chicago, they whisked me through a hallway and shuffled me onto a makeshift wooden dance floor, where my mom was standing with the *America's Got Talent* marquee in the background. She gave me the warmest hug and cried and said, "You know how much I love you, right?"

I teared up, too. "Yes, Mom. Of course I know."

———————

We celebrated my audition that night over Italian food, and my mom left town a day or two later. I had to finish my run of *Oklahoma!*, so I just decided to put the competition out of my mind. As soon as *Oklahoma!* was over, money would become scarce—I didn't have any opera jobs lined up. To make ends meet, I was working two different catering jobs, singing for extra cash at a synagogue in the Gold Coast and a Catholic church in Lincoln Park, and making pop-up performances at a neighborhood Italian restaurant called Viaggio. I was also a new member of the Grant Park Chorus, which performed in Chicago's Millennium Park over the summers. Not to mention I was training for the Ride for AIDS from Chicago to Michigan and back.

With my mind focused on juggling these various jobs, I was taken off guard one day when, after spending the afternoon at Lake Michigan with my dog, I received an email with details about the next stage of the competition: Las Vegas.

My lack of work and income felt insignificant compared to all of the excitement that rushed through me. I immediately hopped on the phone and made my arrangements. Over the next two weeks, I prepared furiously and canceled all of my commitments to spend a week in Vegas. I just decided to blindly trust this journey and pulled out of the Grant Park Chorus altogether. The director, although taken back by my ballsy move, was supportive and understanding.

Much to my delight, when I got to Las Vegas, I was fast-tracked to the next round of the competition, the quarterfinals. This meant that the only thing I had to do was go onstage and express my excitement when my name was called as someone who would go straight through to the live rounds. I never had to perform in Las Vegas. There were only a few of us competitors afforded this luxury.

But while I was at Planet Hollywood, I met my immediate competition. There was a young gay tenor who had been abandoned by his family. Sound familiar? There was Forte, an operatic trio of accomplished singers. Lastly, there was a male soprano named Travis Pratt who sang "O Mio Babbino Caro" from the opera *Gianni Schicchi* in the female key. He proposed to his girlfriend at his audition, and when I watched it on TV and saw how his video went viral, I thought for sure he could win the competition. He never made it out of Sin City.

On my way out to the airport, I met the trio, Forte. It consisted of Puerto Rican tenor Fernando Varela, Metropolitan Opera tenor Sean Panikkar, and classical crossover singer Joshua Page. All of them had large careers in their own right. Seeing them together, I realized how incredible it was that I was being sent straight to Radio City in NYC. When I left Las Vegas, I had a good feeling that the show had big plans for me.

In July I had an *AGT* viewing party at Viaggio, the Italian restaurant just around the corner from where I lived in Chicago. It's a funny thing, becoming a public figure overnight. I hadn't seen any of the footage or heard the storyline the producers had put together about my initial audition until it aired right in front of me and thirty of my friends. I had started a Facebook fan page, a Twitter account, and an Instagram account. After my audition aired, I watched my social media numbers skyrocket into the thousands overnight. My in-box and Twitter feed were flooded with messages and posts from people around the country and beyond, thanking me for sharing my story. I received personal messages from kids who were younger than me—fourteen, fifteen, sixteen, twenty years old. Many had been completely abandoned or kicked out of their homes. Some claimed their parents had abused them; others expressed their fears about coming out.

These messages affected me, profoundly. I couldn't believe the impact I had on other people by simply sharing my own struggles. A young girl named Josie, for example, had been bound in stirrups on suicide watch after attempting to take her own life and was watching in the hospital when my audition came on TV. She claims I saved her life. Josie now follows James and me all over the country to our various shows. No matter what happened from there on out, I was already a winner because of the impact I had been blessed to make.

Of course, I also received a few hate messages, and messages from people who were upset at my mom for her perceived rejection of her son. I learned to look past these comments and messages. A mother of another contestant reminded me that reading those vitriolic comments was like drinking a cup of poison. What was the point?

I made it through three more rounds of the competition, singing "You Raise Me Up," a Spanish cover of "Alone" by the rock band Heart, and Leonard Cohen's "Hallelujah," which landed me in the finals. On the performance night of the finals round of *AGT*, President Barack Obama interrupted live television to give a speech about the Syrian conflict during the first half of its airing. We were warned this planned speech might disrupt some live telecasts of the show. Not surprisingly, the first six acts to compete were voted off the show, and the second six acts made it through to the finale.

I had woken up that morning with a terrible sore throat and made an emergency appointment with an ENT in Manhattan, who told me I had mild vocal strain. He put me on prednisone so I could sing through the competition. When it came time for eliminations, even with the sore throat and the interrupted telecast, I was still truly surprised by the outcome. I had seemed like such a popular candidate, I just found it shocking when I was suddenly voted off.

But as my mom said, she wasn't surprised that I was voted off. She just didn't know if America was ready to embrace a story like mine, especially middle America. Imagine if she'd known I was HIV positive? I wonder what she would have said about that.

I honestly wasn't expecting to be so disappointed when I was voted off. At the final results show, I stood there, alone, as Nick Cannon announced who was advancing and who was going home. When I was escorted off the show set by a production assistant, I realized that I wouldn't really get a chance to say goodbye to anyone I had met on the show. I suppose it made sense—the six remaining acts who made it to the finale were whisked off to film at a dinner with the judges. I, meanwhile, just left the building and walked back to my Hilton hotel room to pack for my morning pickup. It couldn't have been more anticlimactic. I ignored all of my friends' and family's phone calls and just buried my head in the sand for a few days.

But despite my disappointment that it had ended, my experience with the show did have other wonderful effects. There was a great deal of healing that occurred in my family as a result of *America's Got Talent*. My mom, dad, and I were finally able to make amends after being at odds for more than fourteen years. My oldest brother, Jason, sent my mom an email saying how touched he was to see that I was such a kind and sensitive young man. That gift alone was invaluable.

It was as if seeing me through the lens of a television screen was the way my family could finally reconcile their love for me with their views on my sexuality. They needed a buffer to help them truly hear my story. That buffer ended up being a TV show. I never thought reality TV would be the serum that would heal our relationships. But they made immense sacrifices for me during this process, which allowed me to trust them much more than I had in the past. I started to see beyond my own filter and realize just how pure their intentions were for me—at all times.

I had been caught up in my own trauma from my illness, my missteps, and my regrets. I'd spent years blaming them for things they'd already been absolved of. But they'd proved their love time and time again: this time it was me who needed to change. After the show, I was able to see my parents as friends and confidants, and in the process, see just how lucky I was to have them.

CHAPTER
SEVENTEEN

My sudden fame heralded the next stage of personal power in my life, and it brought many changes with it. At home in Chicago, just a couple of months after I was voted off the show, I was finally fed up with the conflicts with Taylor, and I decided I would have to end our relationship. I had started to see my own value, and in the process, I realized he didn't. I returned to Chicago and went straight back to my contract at Lyric Opera of Chicago. Unfortunately, I had to put in one more year as a chorister in order to elect to extend my COBRA health insurance after resigning, if that's what I chose to do. My health insurance had to be my priority. I could have quit and slowly amassed a tour, using the show as a launching pad, but I needed to keep my HIV meds coming.

It was a bizarre sensation walking back into rehearsals for Verdi's *Otello* after having had my fifteen weeks of fame on the most popular network show of the summer. I didn't feel like I belonged there anymore, having had such an enormous solo experience, and I was three weeks behind in music rehearsals. On my commute into work, I was often asked for autographs and photos on the street. People would tell me they believed I got robbed and I should have won. Then I'd put on a burlap sack and become one of eighty peasants in the chorus of the sparse opera production.

My heart wasn't in it anymore. After having a taste of the commercial spotlight, I wanted nothing more than to be out there, recording and touring.

The most common questions I get about the show, even to this day are: *What was it like to be on a show like that? Did the TV show help your career?* I always tell people the experience was a bit like being in a video game and a crazy dream at the same time. Intense pressure, high emotions, high stakes. I wanted to run away as much as I wanted to be there, right up until the day I was voted off. But I'm grateful for having been given the opportunity. It's sort of like winning the lottery: there are exceptionally talented singers in every bar across America, and I was lucky enough to be chosen by the judges. And now there was something burning inside me that told me there was more out there for me.

Having come to understand that my connection with Taylor was corrosive, I finally separated from him. But it wasn't easy. In those first months back in Chicago, I was visibly depressed. Oddly, I had never felt less talented than I did during that time. I felt as if I had failed. I just kept hearing Nick Cannon say over and over, "I'm sorry, Branden. This is the end of the road for you." I believed it, and it nearly ruined me.

But I started seeing a new psychiatrist, who changed my antidepressant and increased the dosage. That seemed to help temporarily—I dropped some weight and had a little more energy—but it wasn't a solid fix. Meanwhile, I got a call to sing "The Prayer" with Jackie Evancho for an event honoring Barbra Streisand in Los Angeles. I had exhausted all of my personal vacation days and had to say no. I said no to many, many gig offers after *AGT* because of my obligations to the opera. Eventually, the calls just stopped coming in.

In April of 2014, after spending three months postbreakup in the same bed as Taylor, I gathered my dignity, moved out of my apartment in Chicago, and put everything I wanted to keep into a storage unit. I flew home to Los Angeles to explore some options and, eventually, made a permanent decision to resign from the opera. I mustered up a few gigs and immersed myself in the Hollywood scene, singing regularly on Monday nights at the Crustacean in Beverly Hills, where David Foster would often attend. I bought a car, drove for Uber and Lyft for a bit, and went on an occasional date here and there. Living back in my friends' guesthouse in West Hollywood, where I'd spent a year or two in my twenties, I felt like a failure. I felt as if I had abandoned my dog, Dolly, and I missed the comforts of being in a relationship.

But being alone without a relationship to exist in, alone with my waffling confidence, still carried one advantage—I was able to face how difficult it was for me to be by myself. After taking an objective look at my previous relationships, I realized how codependent I was, and I sought further psychiatric help. My experience on the show made me realize that I still had something to say and lives to touch. And most importantly, I still needed to find myself. In the process of looking for help, I was introduced to something called the Landmark Forum.

I was desperate and lonely and broke, but I still had a

fighting spirit in me somewhere. The Landmark Forum ended up being transformational for me. Many argue that it is a gimmick, but at the core of its corporate approach to life coaching, there is a great amount of value in its courses. The teachings of the Landmark Forum reminded me how much value we place on the meaning of our lives and what we want to be remembered for. But at the end of the day, none of that matters. Life should be lived in the present, and we should focus on what's happening now, rather than worrying so much about what may happen in the future or what happened in the past. I started to see what a waste of time it was to fixate on shame and regret.

These were new concepts for me. I only knew how to live in a swath of guilt and shame—as a Christian, as a gay man, and as a disgraced HIV-positive man. I honestly had never considered living in the present, as strange as that may sound. As a Christian, because the doctrine tells us that we're not here for this life, but only to prepare for our eternal lives in heaven, I was taught *only* to focus on my future— in my case, a worrisome future. As a gay man, shamed by his church and his family, I was also never able to escape regret, which meant I lived in the past a great deal. This tendency—to worry about the future and regret the past—had only become worse when I was diagnosed with HIV.

At the Landmark Forum, though it was a challenging new way to see my life, I continued my brave and bold ways, and on day three of the five-day seminar, I stood up in front of 250 strangers and told them all my story and how ashamed I was of my condition. Again, speaking the truth saved me. That weekend changed my life. In those three days, I forgave myself for contracting HIV, I forgave my family for our shared lack of understanding, and I forged a way to truly love myself for the first time, by taking responsibility for my own life.

As I finally shared the part of me I had kept hidden for so long, I realized that we are the ones who have control over our own experiences. Of course, depression and hardships can be circumstantial, but in the end, it's up to each of us to fix the areas of our life we aren't happy with. I had always been told to *let go and let God* . . . But this way of thinking meant that my life was in total disarray, because I was still waiting for God to fix everything for me. It had only led to silence, to waiting, and to frustration that things hadn't worked out the way I'd hoped.

My new freedom of loving myself brought with it immediate returns. Within a matter of weeks, and just eight months after moving to Los Angeles, I had plenty of work coming in. Then, by complete accident, I met my husband and my soul mate on an online dating app. He just happened to be a cellist, pianist, and music arranger—not to mention a handsome Australian man of faith who values his family, friends, and most importantly, himself.

Once you've lived a fraudulent life, whether chosen or not, and then you make a conscious effort to change that lifestyle, it becomes so much easier to see through other people's bullshit. When James and I first moved in together, we rented the bottom floor of a gorgeous, three-story Japanese-style house, which was just adjacent to Hollywood. We loved the house, especially the twelve-person Jacuzzi/pool and the fire pit that were in our backyard, not to mention the koi pond in the front yard. It was built up in the hills among a smattering of eucalyptus and pine trees. We fondly referred to it as our tree house. It was one of those ridiculous deals you find in LA only once in a blue moon, and we were in heaven. But after a few months of living there, I came home from my morning Uber-driving shift to find a three-page notice of foreclosure taped on the fence. I took some photos of the notice and sent it to my landlord. He said, "Don't worry about it. Those are just tacky lawyers trying to scare people into changing their homeowner's insurance policies."

I found the response to be suspect, so I put on my best Nancy Drew hat and started digging. It was obvious to me that he was lying. It had been a long time since I was taken for a fool by the phony music producer and acting manager, and now I was much wiser. I was determined that this time around, Hollywood wouldn't take me for a ride. I realized after some careful research that the landlord had just bought a brand-new house on the other side of town. In fact, the day he decided to move out of his current house, he left everything there with it. I mean, everything—his dirty laundry still sat in his hamper, his closet was full of clothes, his financial files and medications still lived in their designated places. Not to mention he left every piece of furniture behind and even photos of his loved ones on the walls. When I called him out on his delinquencies, he produced a letter on Chase Bank letterhead from a branch manager stating he had always been in good standing since his mortgage loan began four years previously.

Being the sleuth that I was, I took the letter into Chase Bank and handed it to the branch manager. He told me the letter was a fake and that he'd have to confiscate it. With more investigation, I noticed the house was scheduled for auction in three weeks' time. Then, one warm morning, while we were enjoying our oatmeal on our top deck, James and I heard a commotion in the garage. It was a team of people who had seen that our house was on a foreclosure list and decided to ransack the place. When I informed them that the house was still occupied, they scurried away as fast as they could. It took us a while to realize they had stolen the large flat-screen TV that Greg Louganis had given to us when he moved out of his Malibu house. We were under siege in the home we rented. I filed a police report and handed things over to the LAPD.

We decided to say goodbye to the tree house, even though we loved it so much. Word on the street was my landlord's parents bailed him out, and he was able to salvage his mortgage and turn a profit on his house. Only in LA, folks—only in LA.

My husband and I share a fairy-tale life now, having traveled to more than thirty-five countries together professionally, playing our own creative musical arrangements for audiences large and small. We refer to each other as sync buddies, because we say and do things simultaneously on a daily basis. It's downright scary how much we're alike. We're asked if we are brothers almost daily. I think, like many dog owners who look like the animals they own, we too have taken on traits from one another.

It's a fragile position to be in, when you both live and work full-time with your partner. Lucky for us, we're the best of friends. Our lives aren't always glamorous, traveling on multiple-leg flights for up to twenty-six hours in economy or sharing a tiny cabin in a ship's crew quarters with two giant cellos. But what we do share is a love for music and travel that fills our life with abundance. For that, I am the most blessed man on the planet.

Having success as a musical duo with my husband has been the greatest gift I've received in my life. Our musical pairing was unlikely. I picked up a job in a piano bar in Santa Fe, New Mexico, to generate more income and try something different. A few weeks into my first contract, James brought his cello and joined me, and we created new arrangements together, based on the requests of the patrons in the bar. From the moment we first played our tango version of "Hotel California," people were transfixed by our connection on stage and the love we share for one another, which shines high above everything else.

Without ever trying, we created a unique sound, and our natural cohesion has been a source of great joy for many people. We owe everything we have to the people in Santa Fe who embraced us even before we knew who we were as artists. The locals have a saying that goes like this: "You don't choose to come to Santa Fe. It chooses you." I didn't choose music; it chose me. I didn't choose authenticity; it chose me. You can plan your whole life within an inch, but it's probably not going to work out that way.

After *America's Got Talent*, I eventually found that promoters, producers, agents, managers, and music directors did start taking me a little more seriously, now that I was in the public eye. The show ultimately opened many, many doors for me. I've collaborated with several former contestants from the show and have been asked to perform with some rather legendary names simply because of the brand I carry with me. I've used those opportunities to further my career with James—recording new albums, making music videos, going on tour in new countries. It's a far cry from singing in a burlap sack in the back of a chorus, and so much better than I could have ever hoped for.

The biggest dream come true is that now I've carved out a niche for myself in a very unique duo—with my husband. We travel around the world living out our dreams, together. There are very few people in this world who can say that.

———————————

On February 13, 2015, I told my parents that I was HIV positive. I invited them up from Orange County to our house in Silverlake to celebrate their anniversary with them. The morning after their celebrations, with James by my side, I shared my story with my parents in our kitchen over a cup of coffee. A single tear ran down my mom's face. She stared blankly at the wall while I told her the story.

But my dad, incredibly, went on a crusade in favor of his son. He said, "I'm going to get a bumper sticker that says, 'My son has HIV and I'm proud of him,' and drive my car around Orange County for everyone to see. To hell with them!" he exclaimed. My father has always had a humorous and nutty way of reacting to serious situations, but it was such a change from the relationship we'd had fifteen years before. All of the fear and worry I carried left my body. My parents were the last people I needed to tell about my HIV status, and also the most difficult to tell. But my life had changed dramatically since that day at the clinic in Los Angeles. And nearly a dozen years later, my dad had changed as well.

My mom called me a few days later and asked me to share all of the details with her again. She was so distracted and upset by my news that she hadn't been able to pay attention to the details the first time. She wasn't ashamed of me or disappointed in me for what I was sharing. She was sad, rather, that I had kept this information from them for eleven years. She regretted not being more of a trustworthy person back then. My parents have transformed themselves, as have I. More recently, my mom said to me, "Every time I think about your HIV status, I'm in disbelief. It still doesn't feel real to me." I reminded her that I share the same feeling: I'm happy and healthy now, thanks to breakthroughs in medications, the advent of PrEP, and my parents' love and forgiveness. I often go for months without thinking about my condition, because it just doesn't carry the same weight it once did.

As for religion, I'm still skeptical of the church as a whole. But as far as God is concerned? God was always there for me and will continue to guide me through all that is seen and unseen. That's why, without any reservation, I can proudly call myself a Christian. My parents gave me my faith, and it is my faith that has saved me time and time again.

At the lowest point of my despair after the show, on a cold December day in Chicago, I was riding my bicycle to the opera. There was a large city bus hovering just behind me. For a fleeting second, I considered pulling in front of that bus and ending my life. I thought anything might be better than the pain I was in at that moment.

But then I thought about Josie, who is healthy and thriving and inspired *because of me*. I thought of my family, who loves me without condition—even the ones who disagree with me. I thought of all the gifts music has brought to my life. My friend Maya said to me once, "You'll know when it's time to leave." As much as I wanted my pain to end, I knew it wasn't time to leave.

Fear and guilt and shame had me in their grips for the better part of my life, but now I understand that they only had power when I wasn't living my truth.

I dared to be authentic and transparent on TV, and afterward, I learned to love myself with the help of a life-coaching seminar whose doctrine was exactly that: to remain in the present and live a life of authenticity. These were things I never knew I needed and never anticipated finding. Life is guaranteed to take us in the most unexpected directions. Some paths we choose, and others are clearly chosen for us by divine guidance or sheer providence.

As for my self-esteem, every day is still a challenge. I'd be lying if I said I don't struggle. Amanda Palmer, who wrote a brilliant book called *The Art of Asking*, calls that struggle the "fraud police." It's the little voices in your head that tell you you're not good enough or worthy enough. Regardless of how I'm feeling or what trajectory of success I'm on, I realize those voices will never completely go away. I've learned to ignore them, for the most part. Every once in a while, my lack of self-confidence will rear its ugly head and I'll be back at baseline again: feeling like the most talentless person on Earth. That's just who I am, and it's also the plight of many artists.

But I'm much happier than I ever was before. Life continues to bless me in the most beautiful ways. I've managed to shut down that voice in my head that would be so quick to criticize and judge previously. I still like a glass of wine or two, and I've used edible marijuana in places where it's legal, but I don't use these things for escapism anymore. I've learned to try and be content with my state of mind, no matter what it is. Life ebbs and flows for all of us. I'm working on my awareness of this slowly, through meditation and mindfulness.

I've faced adversity in my life, but it does not define me. It has only made me more daring, more empathetic. It has given me humility and character and made me a great deal wiser. I never saw it coming that I'd be asked to write a memoir. It was never anything I aspired to do. I started blogging because my social media adviser told me it would improve my search engine optimization. But I realized while penning those blog posts that my story, although rather common, is not a story that people share often. My hardships, setbacks, and trauma cannot compare to what others have endured in their own lives, but pain *is* still real and relative for all of us who experience it.

Now, it's my responsibility to share my stories, my shortcomings, and the lessons I've learned with all who need to hear them. There is so much more to who we are than what we post on Facebook. Living a life of authenticity and transparency is the key to personal freedom. I believe if we all subscribed to this commitment to authenticity, we'd all understand one another a bit more. We'd realize how similar we are, rather than believing the naysayers who say we're different and divided.

Back on that fateful day in 2013 in Chicago, I started a conversation about the importance of being open and transparent and wearing our scars with pride. Now I intend to finish it.